ANCIENT EGYPTIANS AND CHINESE IN AMERICA

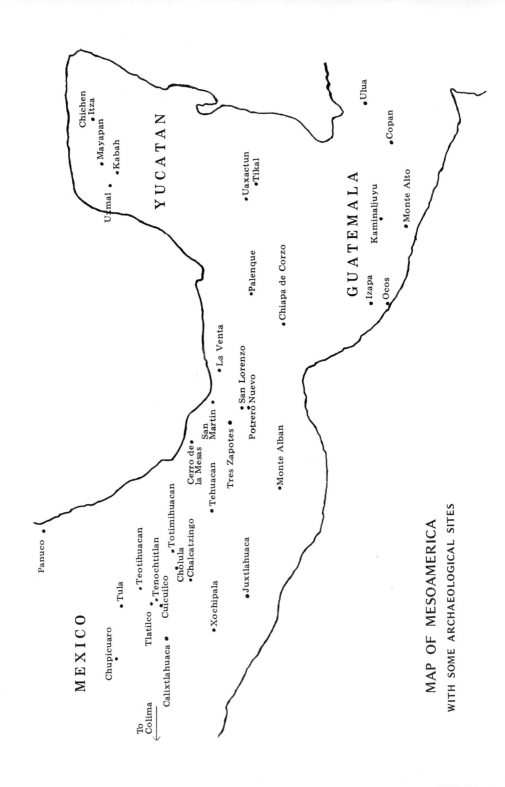

MAP OF MESOAMERICA

WITH SOME ARCHAEOLOGICAL SITES

MEXICO

Panuco •

Chupicuaro •

• Tula

Tlatilco • • Teotihuacan

Calixtlahuaca • Cuicuilco • • Tenochtitlan

Cholula • • Totimihuacan

Chalcatzingo •

Cerro de la Mesas •

San Martin • • La Venta

• Tehuacan • San Lorenzo

Tres Zapotes • Potrero Nuevo •

Xochipala •

• Monte Alban

Juxtlahuaca •

To Colima

YUCATAN

Chichen Itza •

Mayapan •

Uxmal • • Kabah

• Palenque

• Chiapa de Corzo

• Uaxactun • Tikal

GUATEMALA

• Ulua

• Copan

Kaminaljuyu •

• Monte Alto

Izapa • Ocos •

ANCIENT EGYPTIANS

AND CHINESE

IN AMERICA

R. A. JAIRAZBHOY

GEORGE PRIOR ASSOCIATED PUBLISHERS LTD.
LONDON

*Dedicated to the Mexican people who preserved
the inheritance of the Old World and made it anew.*

First published in 1974 by George Prior Publishers,
Rugby Chambers, 2 Rugby Street, London WClN 3QU

ISBN   0 904000 01X

Printed in England by
Pika Print Limited, 76 Graeme Road, Enfield, Middlesex

CONTENTS

Preface and Acknowledgement   6

Chapter III A   **Ancient Egyptians civilise America**   7

       Part 1   **The Egyptians in Mexico**   7

            2   **The Migrants and their Races**   17

            3   **Institutions and Customs**   28

            4   **Art and Culture**   35

            5   **Rituals**   43

            6   **Egyptian Gods in Mexico**   49

            7   **Egypt's Underworld in Mexico**   67

            8   **Continued search for Paradise**   83

            9   **The Egyptian haven in Titicaca**   92

Chapter III B   **Refugees from China**   100

Appendix   **Pyramid and Mound**   113

Bibliography   121

PREFACE

It is my belief that the high civilisations of ancient America are the result of an amalgam of ideas from the Old World - modified, extended and continued by the genius of the New. At the core lies the imported heritage. This book, therefore, has a new (some may think a revolutionary) viewpoint, as it sets out to discover what were the roots that nourished Mesoamerica, and to a lesser extent Peru.

The present volume constitutes chapter 3 of the work "Old World Origins of American Civilization". It was decided to uproot and modify this chapter, and publish it first because of economic reasons, its intrinsic importance in relation with the whole, and because it can stand on its own. Moreover whereas the rest of the work relies to a certain extent on the existing literature, the present volume is almost entirely based on original research and interpretation. The author is acutely aware of the vast strides being made in the understanding of early America through excavation, and he knows that some of the evidence and dating will require modification in the years to come when the rich sites have yielded their secrets.

The reactions of different persons in reading part or whole of this work in an earlier draft varied considerably. Nevertheless I am grateful to them all - to Professor Arnold Toynbee for his kind encouragement, the late Professor Paul Kirchhoff for caution and criticism, Dr. Ignacio Bernal for scepticism and courtesy, Miss Ann Kendall for expressing the other side of the coin, C.E. Joel for comments and corrections, Eduardo Martinez for photographic help, Mr. C.A. Burland and Professor George F. Carter for some suggestions, and above all to Gerhard Kraus for confidence and support all along the way.

ACKNOWLEDGEMENT

I would like to thank the following for their kind permission to reproduce illustrations in this book:
The Oriental Institute, University of Chicago for Ills. 7, 45, 79; The Metropolitan Museum of Art (anon. gift 1931) for Ill. 24; Yale University Press (after An Chih Min and Wu Ju-tso, KKP, 1957/2, pp.5, 8) for Ill. 113; Dr. Ignacio Bernal for Ill. 25; Dr. Cheng Te K'un for Ill. 103b; Dr and Mrs. Josue Saenz for Ill. 46; Brown University Press, Providence, Rhode Island for Ill. 92; Editions Payot, Paris for Ill. 8; *Archeologia,* Paris (C. Remy) for Ill. 103a; Lambert Schneider GmbH, Heidelberg for Ill. 64; Alfred A. Knopf Inc., New York for Ills. 34 and 14. Ills. 44, 60, and 86 were drawn from V. Garth Norman. Finally reprinted by permission of Princeton University Press are the following from the works of A. Piankoff published by Bollingen Foundation: *The Tomb of Rameses VI,* 1954, p.174, pls. 113, 187, fig. 54; *The Shrines of Tut-Ankh-Amon,* 1955, pp.28-29; *Mythological Papyri,* 1957, figs. 25, 70.

PART 1

The Egyptians in Mexico

In some uncanny manner the memory of man is able to span millennia. Nowhere is this better exemplified than in ancient Mexico. Nothing could erase from the memory of the Pre-Columbian Indian the fact that his ancestors had come to this land from some far-away place across the seas. All the accounts are unanimous as we shall see. Clearly in the face of the native accounts we are not justified either in doubting their veracity or in ignoring them.

The Olmecs burst in on the Mexican Gulf in about 1200 B.C.—this much is generally agreed. Before their appearance there were villages and pottery in Mexico, but not a great deal more. After the appearance of the Olmecs all kinds of civilised activity appears including massive organisation of labour, a trade network, ceremonial centres with pyramids, colossal sculpture, relief carving, wall painting, orientation of structures, gods and religious symbolism, an obsession with the Underworld, representations of foreign racial types, hieroglyphic writing and scribes, seals and rings, use of iron, and so on. Most of what appears in this context is not obviously Egyptian in appearance, or it would have been detected at once.

There are a number of reasons why the transmitted traits are different from their prototypes, as analysis reveals. Here are some of them: 1. As we shall see the migrants were of various ethnic types — Egyptians, Negroes, Semites, and Chinese. 2. There is a preponderance of traits to do with the Underworld, since their journey seems to have been motivated by the purpose of discovering its entrance which was imagined to be in the Far West of the World. 3. The accident of excavation and discovery. Few artifacts so far found seem to go back to the first generation migrants. In succeeding generations after inter-marrying with the natives there was progressive deviation and addition to the imported culture. The sons of the migrants did not have the Old World models in their memory, for they had never seen them at first hand. 4. The removal of conventional constraints and law allowed ideas to be extended freely in new directions. 5. The response to a new environment. These are some of the reasons why a replica of Egyptian civilisation was not transplanted onto Mexican soil.

Nevertheless, probably through a surviving generation of priests, a large number of traits endured in Mexico long after Pharaonic civilisation had ceased in Egypt. With a little perception the modified ideas can be linked with their source.

What I shall point to are not stray influences, but a sudden influx of civilisation at a given moment in time. And this is exactly corroborated by native accounts which recollected the memory of the event right up to the coming of the Spaniards.

Here is what the Aztec King Montezuma said to the Spanish conqueror Cortes: "For a long time and by means of our writings, we have possessed a knowledge transmitted from our ancestors, that neither I nor any of us who inhabit this land are of native origin.

We are foreigners and came here from very remote parts. We possess information that our lineage was led to this land by a lord to whom we all owed allegiance. He afterward left this for his native country . . . but, we have ever believed that his descendants would surely come here to subjugate this land and us who are, by rights, their vassals.

Because of what you say concerning the region whence you come, which is where the sun rises, . . . we believe and hold as certain that he (the Spanish King) must be our rightful lord". *(MacNutt, F.A.: 1908, I, p.234).*

And here is what that most respected authority Father Benardino de Sahagun says: "Concerning the origin of this people the account which the old people give is that they came by sea from toward the north, and it is certain that they came in some vessels of wood, but it is not known how they were built; but it is conjectured by one report which there is among all these natives, that they came out of seven caves, and that these seven caves are the seven ships or galleys in which the first settlers of this land came, as is inferred from the truthful conjectures. The first people to settle the land came from toward Florida, and they came along the coast, and disembarked at the port of Panuco (north of Veracruz) which they call Panco, which means, place where those who crossed the water arrived. These people came looking for a terrestrial paradise, and they settled near the highest mountains they found." *(Sahagun: 1946, pp. 13-14; Sorenson, 1955, p.429).*

The two accounts taken together can be harmonised with the evidence presented in this chapter with very little difficulty. (The problem of the ships coming from toward Florida is easily solved if we recall that Florida is due West of Egypt. The voyage continued past because there was a further horizon beyond, and they followed the curve of the Gulf till they could go no further West.) One of the most intriguing questions raised is the reference of the seven galleys. It is a clear indication that the immigrants did not come singly, but in a substantial fleet. And the fact of there being seven ships involved could be significant, for in the tomb of Rameses III a room inscribed with the text "Litany of the Sun" has a ceiling with seven ships amid the stars. *(Lefébure, M.E.: 1889, pp. 91-2; Champollion: 1945, III, pl. CCLVI; Rosellini, J.: 1832-44, II, pls. 107, 108.)*

The *Popol Vuh*, the Epic of the Quiche Maya of Guatemala, has a similar account: the ancestors decide to set out in search (5237-8), hear news of a city, and go there (5247-8). "Seven caves, seven canyons was the name of the city" (5259-60), and they all arrive at Tula (5263). I shall endeavour to show (p.67f) that the city they were seeking was the Egyptian paradisal city Iaru, confirming what Sahagun had said—that the first people who came by sea "came looking for a terrestial paradise".

8

It might be queried how the Aztecs and Mayas could be expected to have the same traditions about their ancestors. The answer is that ancestral to them both were the Olmecs who had spread in both areas and made settlements there. Another question is—how could one be sure that the *Popol Vuh* refers to really ancient times when it purports to trace the Quiche ancestry only 13 generations back which could take it back to a date somewhere in the region of c.1303 AD *(Wauchope: 1948, pp. 38-39)* since it was compiled in its present form in c.1555. The answer to this is that the solar mythology and overseas migration depicted in the text, the jaguar cult, and the actual name of the ancestors, all can be traced back to the Egypto-Olmecs (as I call them hereafter). I now elaborate these points.

In a long passage relating to the Fourth Creation, the *Popol Vuh* (5050f.) is clearly talking about the very earliest times. And at the end of it (7221f.), it declares that these people "were the first men to come from there across the sea from the sunrise. Long ago then they came here. Sacrificers and worshippers they were called".

The Olmecs had "a highly developed priesthood" *(Heizer: 1971, p.61)*, and I shall show below (p.49f) that their whole pantheon is of Egyptian origin. Indeed before the appearance of the Olmecs, as far as we know at present, there were no specific deities worshipped in the Americas, or at least there were no images of them. The Olmecs should therefore deservedly be called "sacrificers and worshippers".

As for being "sacrificers", what could this have involved? Elsewhere the *Popol Vuh* describes (6375f.) how the Tribes kept disappearing in ones and twos, and were later discovered flayed, cut and sacrificed. When they found such a victim they assumed "Jaguar is eating", and were convinced that sacrifices were being made before the ancestors. Thus far there is no certain evidence that human sacrifice was being practised in Olmec times, but from the V-cleft on the skulls of representations of jaguars (e.g. in Ill. 18 and 65) it seems that the jaguar was being ritually slaughtered with an axe. An Olmec relief (Ill. 1) represents a priest directing a were-jaguar baby to wield an axe. A Maya effigy has an axe emerging from its forehead *(Greene, M. et al: 1972, p.32)*. The question is how did such a practice arise? Possibly because the Egyptian word for perforating the skull—*thm*, was the same one which meant "to travel with the dead in the Underworld" *(Breasted, J.H.: 1930, pp. 126-7)*, and it may be this dual sense that was implied by the mummies of Ramessid rulers having holes on the back of their skull *(Elliot Smith and Dawson, W.R.: 1925, fig. 27, pp. 100, 105)*. Alternatively there is in the 5th Division of the Egyptian Underworld a goddess called "lives upon the blood of the dead" *(Budge: 1906, pp. 109, 113)*. She is steadying the axe with which a self-inflicted wound is being executed. (Ill. 2) An Egyptian hieroglyph consisting of a man directing an axe at his own head meant death and to die, and this was used especially in the context of prisoner or enemy *(Gardiner: 1915, p. 21)*. Thus if the Olmecs did practice sacrifice of their enemies by inflicting cranial wounds, the Egyptian antecedents outlined above should be taken into account in tracing the origins of the Mesoamerican practice.

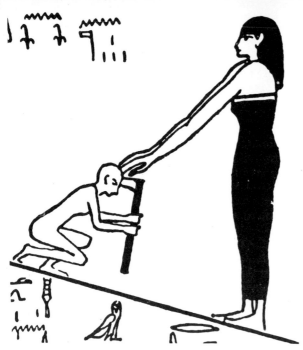

2. Egyptian sacrificial act — Person wielding axe at own head directed by goddess — means "death" or "to die" in Egyptian hieroglyph.

1. Olmec relief (Parque la Venta, Villa-hermosa) Priest carrying jaguar-baby, is wielding an axe — presumed sacrificial act.

In another place, the *Popol Vuh* (5065, 5089) calls the ancestors from the sunrise "the Branches and Seers". The latter may be imagined to have consisted of scribes and priests—their presence is everywhere evident in the Olmec context. But why anyone should be called Branches *(Tam)* was at first baffling. Eventually from the third division of the Egyptian *Book of What is in the Underworld* came an explanation. One of the boats represented here is called "the Branch" (Pa-khet), and each end of the boat terminates in the head of a lion (Ill. 3) *(Budge: 1906; I, pp. 47-8)*. I shall show below (p. 70) that much of the Mexican conception of the Underworld stems from this very book. I conclude therefore that the Branches must have been the crew of a boat named after the Underworld boat called "the Branch", particularly since the expedition had been sent to explore the Underworld. If my identification is correct, it explains one more mystery of the Olmecs who constantly resorted to the use of the jaguar mask, for once lionhead terminals had identified their ship. And again in the Underworld stages as represented in *Codex Vaticanus A* it is the head of a jaguar which is crossing the sea before the entrance to the Underworld is reached. (Ill. 4).

I had long ago concluded that the ancestors came in search of the sun; that is to say they were hoping to follow the sun into the Underworld so that they could be united with it at its rising. The *Popol Vuh* (5231) says that their ancestors "just wore their hearts out there in expectation of the sun", and then when they arrive in this land they watched closely for the dawn (5577f.), for the birth of the sun (5851), but they could not perceive what they were looking for, and had to conclude that "this is not our home here". They were saddened that they had become exiled, and disillusioned that their gods had brought them from the sunrise (5888). And they (some?) decide to go away and continue their search (5611).

I maintain that what they were hoping to see was evidence that they had become one with the sun. Sahagun *(1950-63: Bk. 1, pp. 81-4)*, recounting adages in the format of the solar cycle, comes to the dawning of the sun and lastly to the stage "truly thou hast attained the sun". This belief stems from Egypt where texts describe the deceased being "taken up to heaven and united with the sundisc" *(Pritchard: 1955, p. 18)*.

Once again the correspondence between Egyptian and Mexican beliefs about the journey across the sky with the sun to the West is too precise to be a coincidence. In Aztec myth, according to Father Duran, *(Duran, Fray D: 1964, p. 172)* it was believed that the dead would fly before the sun every day, and according to Sahagun *(II, p. 181; Soustelle, J: 1968, pp. 194-5)* the soldiers and the women who died in childbirth go to the sun and live in the western part of the heavens.

4. Stages of the Mexican Underworld from *Codex Vaticanus A*. In stage 2 a jaguar-head is seen crossing the sea with shells.

3. Boat called "the Branch" passing through the third division of the Egyptian Underworld — boat bears terminals representing lion's head (or leopard, equivalent to jaguar/panther).

If Seler is right the Aztec underworld paradise Cincalco is identical with *Tamoanchan* (temoua in chan "the house where they descend"), and he claims that this would "undoubtedly indicate 'a land in the West' where the sun descends to earth" *(Seler, E.: 1900-01, p. 105)*.

We now come to the question of how Egyptian events relate to their Mexican counterparts in time as well as in substance.

When the Egyptian king died, he joined the sun-god Ra in his journey across the sky during the day and through the Underworld at night. Such a journey is described in quite literal terms. There is a chapter in the *Pyramid Texts* entitled "Means whereby the deceased king reaches Heaven". It is described how "two reed floats of heaven are placed for Ra that he may ferry over with these to the horizon" *(Mercer, S.A.B.: 1952, I. p. 86)*. When Pepi II died c.2180 B.C. the texts described how "The inhabitants of the horizon row him" *(ibid, p. 90)*. And it is reiterated "the sailors will take Ra and Pepi round about the horizon" *(ibid, p. 138)*. Pepi purifies himself, sits in the boat and takes the helm. And he is rowed to the West with his panther-skin loin cloth on. He is called "the great helmsman who has voyaged over the two parts of heaven" *(ibid, p. 165)*. There are many indications that Rameses III (c.1195-1164 B.C.) yearned passionately to reach the Western horizon. The text says "When he reaches the district of Manu he is joyful of heart" *(Breasted, J.H.: 1096-07, IV, p. 9)*. In the "Hymn to the Setting Sun", in the *Book of the Dead*, Manu is identified as the mountain of the sunset *(Budge, E.A.W.: 1898, p. 40f.)* And here again is the concluding prayer to Ammon from *Papyrus Harris* compiled at the death of Rameses III by his son, "O God Ammon...... grant thou that I may arrive in safety, landing in peace, and resting in Tazoser like the gods. May I mingle with the excellent souls of Manu . . .". "I have reached the West like Osiris . . . thou has led me to rest by thy side in the Western heavens like all the mysterious gods of the Nether World. *(Breasted, J.H.: 1906-07, IV, pp. 140, 160-2)*.

Rameses III speaks of his Temple at Medinet Habu surviving "Like the mountain of Manu forever". *(Edgerton, W.F. and Wilson J.A.: 1936, p. 9; cf.pp. 107-8)*. And he himself is represented with the august Ba's in Manu adoring the bark of the setting sun *(University of Chicago; Pl. 430)*. One wonders if this mountain Manu, which lay in the Far West at the edge of the Underworld, survives in Maya tradition as Mani, especially since the ancestors of the Tutulxius of Mani are reputed to have come from the river of the Underworld. *(Seler, E.: 1939, II, pt.1, p. 4)*.

A relief at the Funerary Temple of Medinet Habu represents Rameses III paddling in a boat in Iaru, the Underworld paradise *(University of Chicago: 1963, pl. 469)*. Another relief represents Rameses III running along with the ship's gear *(Ibid, pl. 257)*. And his son Rameses IV affirms that "the Ocean and the Great Circuit . . . to the ends of the supports of the sky" are in his father's grasp *(Edgerton and Wilson: 1936, p. 148, cf.p. 152)*. Already in the first Libyan war in the fifth year of his reign (1190 B.C.) Rameses III had said "none escapes him (even to) the ends of the Great Circle (Okeanis, *sn-wr*) *(Breasted, J.H.: 1906-7, IV, p. 25)*. Not only does he boast that Egypt ruled the seas, but he prepared a large navy and sent them to extreme places. "I made *qerer*-ships, *menesh*-ships, and *bari*-ships on the Great Green Sea in order to transport the goods of the land of Djahi (Syria) and of the countries of the ends of the earth for filling (the treasuries of the gods of Egypt) *(Pritchard, J.B.: 1955, p. 260)*. The type of ships mentioned have been translated as warships, galleys and coasters *(Edgerton and Wilson: 1936, p. 54 n. 206)*. And finally an important text in which Rameses III says: "I hewed great galleys and sent them forth into the great *sea of the inverted water*". He then refers to the ships arriving at the country of Punt safely, and coming back laden *(Breasted, J.H.: 1906-7, IV, p. 203)*.

Having now gathered the texts we see the following picture emerging. Rameses yearns to go to the land of Manu on the Western horizon; he sends naval expeditions to the extremities of the earth; and he gives them licence to go into the inverted water. This seems to me to refer on the one hand to that part of the world where the Red Sea stretched out into the expanse of the Indian Ocean, and on the other hand to where the Mediterranean opens out into the Atlantic Ocean. Remember that Queen Hatshepsut (1504 - 1482) had defined her "boundary south stretching to the shores of Punt, and the boundary West to the land of the going down of the Sun". *(Paton, D.: 1916, II, p. 13; cf. Breasted, J.H.: 1906, II, pt. 328)*.

The ancient Egyptians had a dazzling array of ships available to them. They had the longest unbroken experience of sailing and shipbuilding known in antiquity, and by far the largest number of representations are found in their art *(see Boreaux, C.: 1925, and Landstrom, B.: 1970)*. They would have had little difficulty in crossing the Atlantic in many of these.

But what kind of ship would have been sent to the West? We have seen that the deceased king was conceived as sailing to the (Western) horizon on two reed floats. And a reed craft was pictured as the vehicle of the sun *(Hornell, J.: 1946, p. 51)*. But the reed canoe was an ancient craft which survived until the 12th Dynasty largely for fishing purposes *(Clowes, G.S.L.: 1959, p. 8)*. And once much later it was used in the 8th century B.C. by the Ethiopian rulers of Egypt to convey an ambassador about a distance of 100 miles from Pelusium to Gaza *(Isaiah, XVIII, 1-2)*.

The reed boat is also found in different parts of the world and its distribution has been plotted *(Hornell, J.: 1946)*. It could be that its original home was Egypt, but this would be difficult to prove in view of its widespread diffusion. The presence of the reed boat in the Americas led Dr. Thor Heyerdahl to sail the Atlantic in one of them in 1970 to prove that this *could* have been done in ancient times. While the reed boats of Egypt and Peru are not exactly similar, there is no doubt a strong resemblance between the reed floats of the two areas, as was shown long ago *(Breasted, J.H.: 1917, IV, pp. 174f., 255)*. Indeed I shall show in due course (p.98f) that there is a direct link between the reed boats of Egypt and Peru.

13

However, it is historically documented that for distant expeditions the Pharaohs sent only their largest timber-ships. For example, in Hatshepsut's expedition to the spice land, c.1500 B.C. there was a veritable convoy of ships with broad square sails, and they are estimated to have been about 90 feet long and 25 feet broad *(Casson, L.: 1964, pp. 24-5)*. The *Kerer* ships of Rameses III which brought freight to Egypt were 100 cubits long (about 170 feet) *(Marx, E.: 1946, p. 23)*. Although there were 83 vessels attached to the Temple of the Sun god Ammon-Ra at Thebes under Rameses III *(Marx, E.: 1946, p. 22)*, it is likely that if they took one of these for a ritual purpose, the remainder would have consisted of the normal expeditionary ships.

While the chief corroborative evidence for the Egyptian voyage comes from the Mexican side and is set out in the remainder of the book, some key Ramessid themes bolster this evidence from the Egyptian side.

1. Whether or not other Pharaohs represented themselves on the Far West of the World enjoying paradise, Rameses III certainly did (Ill.5).
2. He built a navy which he says he sent to the ends of the world, and it is at this time that the Olmecs spring up on the Mexican Gulf.

5. Symbolic representation at Medinat Habu of Rameses III in Iaru — "fields of peace". Note the cross-in-disc signs above (University of Chicago).

3. A journey across the sky is represented in his tomb involving seven ships, and Mexican tradition reports that their first ancestors came to this land in seven ships.

4. Rameses III speaks of his expedition being sent to "the inverted waters". Also Egyptian papyrus paintings show the sun's ship sailing inverted across the underside of the sky (Ill. 6) *(Piankoff: 1957, I, p. 190, fig. 70)*. This conception of the inverted solar boat, I identify on a very interesting Olmec relief sculpture now at Villahermosa (Ill. 7). The boat with empty cult shrine and reed clumps on prow and stern, is entering the Underworld over the head of a god whom I shall later show from texts symbolised the mountain of the Far West in Egyptian mythology. (see p. 51).

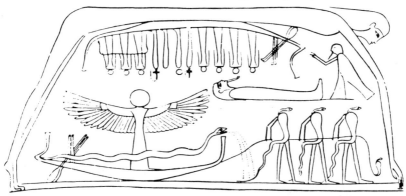

6. Egyptian papyrus painting with solar-boat sailing upside-down on the underside of the sky (Piankoff).

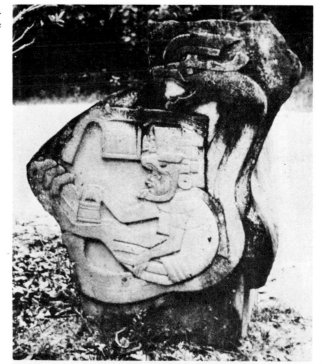

7. Olmec relief (Parque La Venta, Villahermosa). God seated on serpent is overarched by the serpent's head. Note above an upside-down reed boat with crosses.

If I were asked to offer a possible date for the Rameses expedition I would have suggested c.1187 B.C. For a text from this 8th year of his reign speaks of the beauty of the Temple reaching Manu. And in the very next sentence it says "The sun sails to . . . (incomplete)" *(Breasted, J.H.: 1927, IV, p. 8)*. This is as far as the Egyptian evidence can take us. Without the solid evidence of Mexican archaeology as revealed in recent years it would be valueless.

I claim that the new settlers established themselves among other places at the site of San Lorenzo Tenochtitlan in Southern Veracruz. The site had been occupied from about 1500 B.C., and there had been signs of slow change. But in the fourth phase dating from c.1150 B.C., as established by stratified pottery studies and Radio Carbon dating (see Postscript), there was a "mighty cultural upsurge". And in the years that followed "most of the monuments were carved, the site took on something of its present appearance, and population reached an all time high" *(Coe, M.D.: 1970, p. 27)*. In 1968 Michael Coe called the civilisation of the so-called Olmecs "a pristine civilisation" without antecedents and with no earlier models to go by *(Coe, M.D.: 1968a, p. 123)*. But in 1970 he was beginning to admit that "the primary impetus in the establishment of Olmec civilisation there may well have come from some yet-undetected outside area" *(Coe, M.D.: 1970, p. 32)*. Matthew Stirling was clearly puzzled; "One basic mystery remains to be solved. Who were the Olmecs, and what were their antecedents?" *(Stirling, M.W.: 1968, p. 7)*.

I shall now endeavour to clear up the mystery, which I believe largely persists because of the reluctance of Americanists to look outside the continent. The Olmec situation is admittedly also confused by the appearance less than two generations later than Phase I of another great peoples from Asia, with whom I shall deal anon (see p. 100 f.), and whose presence has once again not been suspected.

Postscript

Professor Michael Coe writes (personal communication April 21, 1973) that some adjustments to Olmec chronology will be necessitated by the recent view that C14 dates are too young, and that the beginning of San Lorenzo would thus be mid-15th Century B.C. which would correspond to mid-18th Dynasty Egypt. My response is that *if* the new radio carbon dates indeed achieve a finality along this line, and *if* it can be shown that the specifically Ramessid traits in Mexico (such as penis truncation, the posture of the seated figure in the St. Martin crater, the negro sculptured heads, cranial perforation, the voyage to the inverted waters etc. . . .) are present at an earlier date in Egypt than it appears at the time of writing, then it will become necessary to make adjustments to the conclusions reached by this book.

PART 2

The Migrants and their races

Archaeologists trust the evidence of artifacts implicitly and tend to steer clear of literary texts. The historian must give due weight to both, particularly if he finds that there are points at which the two agree. In reconstructing the New World's ancient past it has not seemed possible until now to link the two kinds of evidence. The present writer has a healthy respect for native annals, and believes that they have much to yield if used with circumspection. This entire work is an attempt to marry up the texts and artifacts. In the previous chapter this approach opened up a new horizon. We saw that Egyptian texts spoke of a journey to the West of the world, the chronology coincided with the appearance of the Olmecs, and the Mexican texts corroborated that the first ancestors who came to this land came across the seas from the rising sun or the east. Other solutions that emerged were explanations for the persistent jaguar cult, the origin of ritual skull sacrifice, and the solar purpose of the voyage. And now we shall turn to the question of the heterogeneous composition of the trans-Atlantic migrants.

Negroes

It is at first disconcerting to find so many different peoples represented in Olmec culture. That the immigrants were a polyglot, multi-racial people is confirmed in the *Popol Vuh*. It says there that the first ancestors who came to this land from the sunrise were "black people, white people, many were the people's looks, many were the people's languages." (5128f.) This is yet another proof of an Egyptian voyage, for nowhere else were there negroes and Semites living together. For example Rameses III lists the Syrians and negroes of the captivity who were serfs of the Temple in Memphis *(Pritchard, J.B.: 1955, p. 261)*. And look at this console from Tanis (Ill.8); it has five heads in a row among which are two Semites, a Libyan, a Nubian and a negro *(Montet, P.: 1942, pl. 2, pp. 50f.)*. Indeed the Olmec idea of carving portrait heads may have come from this very precedent in Egypt. I claim that Tanis must be the very place from which our voyage started for it was the Ramessid Delta capital and was "the harbourage of the ship's troops", from which ships went on distant expeditions. *(Save-Soderberg, T.: 1946, p. 39)*.

When the monolithic Olmec heads were first discovered, they were declared to be negroid. Chavero described the colossal head found in 1860 at Hueyapan around San Andres Tuxtla as an Ethiopian *(Riva Palacio, D.V.: 1877, p. 63)*. But since no explanation was found for

9. Colossal Olmec head with negroid features now in Jalapa Museum. Observe helmet with linear markings.

negroes in ancient America, it is no longer fashionable to speak in this manner now. In view of the Egyptian voyage, the fact of their being negroes once again becomes plausible, for it was commonplace in the New Kingdom to have negro slaves and mercenaries, and it is not straining the imagination to conceive of the crew members of an Egyptian ship consisting of sturdy negro oarsmen, and soldiers (remember that soldiers had been sent in previous expeditions to Punt *(Naville, E.: 1901, pt. 3, p. 19)*. From a later analogy we can see how quickly such negroes might have made their mark in the new habitat, first as soldiers and then as generals. The example comes from the 16th Century A.D. when a party of 16 negroes were shipwrecked off the Esmerelda Coast. "They intermarried with the native women, and in a short time they were able to control the whole province." *(Estrada, E. and Meggers: 1961, p. 936)*. The Olmec heads of which there are now over a dozen, have been described as "tough warrior dynasts" *(Coe, M.D.: 1968a, p. 110)* and I think this is not far off the mark. They indicate a rugged strength and seem to be persons in authority. I would suggest that they were military governors of the new

8. Egyptian heads from Tanis of Ramessid period wearing leather helmets. They portray traditional enemies including negroes (Montet).

found Egyptian colony on the Gulf of Mexico. The colossal heads have two distinct links with Egypt. One is that nowhere in the world at the time were sculptures of this scale being erected than in Egypt. Some of the heads being 6-8 feet high, would have been altogether about 50 feet high had they had bodies. This is almost on the scale of Rameses II at Abu Simbel which are about 65 feet high. The second is that the Olmec heads wear leather helmets, and in Egypt leather helmets were then being made *(Montet, P.: 1958, p. 155)*. The helmet at the time of Rameses III completely covered both the head and the back of the neck *(ibid, p. 231)*. Then there are the tie-ons attached at the crest and falling in front of the ears such as a Lybian prisoner of Rameses III wears at Medinet Habu *(Culican, W.: 1966, p. 69)*. Another fallen enemy at Karnak has double strings *(Description de l'Egypte, 1812, III, pl. 39)*, just as on one of the Olmec heads at the Jalapa Museum (Ill. 9). This helmet has decorative parallel lines incised on it like the Egyptian ones from Tanis. It is possible that these Olmec heads began by being a commemoration of foreign rulers. In time the emphasis may have changed and the heads were then thought of as monuments to dead ancestors. It was this conception that

19

seems to have survived with the Mayas who had the custom of preserving the heads of important people for adoration *(Morley, S.: 1956, p. 206)*.

Apart from the monumental heads there are a number of other Olmec faces which are negroid, some found in excavated contexts, others not. One such, whose authenticity is not suspect is of a so-called acrobat in terracotta from a cemetery of the Olmec period in highland Mexico. It is admitted to have negroid features *(Carmen Aguilera: 1971, fig. 23)*. In fact some skulls at the Tlatilco cemetery were examined by an anthropologist who concluded that they were of heterogeneous type including negroid, and he attributed this to "an extraneous and more or less sporadic trans-Atlantic migration" *(Wierzcinski: 1969)*. This conclusion has been rejected by a respected Mexican anthropologist because of craniometric variability *(Comas, J.: 1972)*. That is to say of 98 crania examined in Tlatilco 13.5% were negroid, and of 25 skulls from Cerro de la Mesas 4.5% were negroid, and while at the former site the females were different, at the latter they are the same as the male. But if the former skulls were of the Pre-classic period and the latter of the Classic, then this is surely what one would expect, since after centuries of intermarriage with the natives the small negro population would have become absorbed. A further attempt to deny that the colossal Olmec heads are negroid is the argument that the thick lips and flattened noses are derived from the features of a jaguar *(Comas, J.: 1973, p. 84f.)*. There certainly are jaguar-like human faces in Olmec art, but the great heads are not conventions but brilliant characterizations of real humans each with his own individuality. Of the other negroid features stated to be absent "woolly hair" is impossible to determine with the heads that wear helmets, though many terracotta heads in Von Wuthenau's collection (1973) do have such hair, and the monumental cratered god also appears to have crinkly hair (see Ill. 55).

It is quite understandable that patriotic Mexican scholars should resist the conclusion that their ancestral culture was ruled by a dynasty of negro rulers who had once been Nubian slaves, and who lorded it over the Gulf of Mexico like aspiring Pharaohs, and like the Pharaohs had their heads carved and towed and rafted far from their quarries. A face may be ambiguous in what its affinities are, but seen against the whole cultural situation sketched in this book, it could allow a more definite conclusion. For this author the conclusion is that the negro started his career in America not as slave but as master.

Semites

It is still premature to identify an actual Egyptian face in Olmec culture. This may be for a combination of reasons such as that there may have been few of them among the ship's personnel (certainly at least the priests and scribes), that there is no easily recognisable characteristic Egyptian type, or that it is simply a case of the accident of discovery. If the physical presence of the Egyptian is not discernible, his cultural presence at any rate looms large in Formative Mesoamerica.

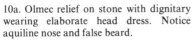
10b. From same relief, figure situated above pointing his index finger at the dignitary.

10a. Olmec relief on stone with dignitary wearing elaborate head dress. Notice aquiline nose and false beard.

The presence of Semites in Mexico is much more demonstrable. An Olmec relief (Ill. 10a) dubbed by the archaeologists "Uncle Sam", depicts a personage with typical aquiline nose and what could be a false beard. He is confronted by a woman, and has an entourage above tilted in a peculiar perspective perhaps on account of the limited lateral space on the boulder on which it is carved. One of the figures above raises his hands, which at first seems to resemble the manner in which the Pharaoh was greeted. But a more careful look reveals that he has the fore-finger of one hand outstretched in a pointing gesture (Ill. 10b), and this emphatically links him with a Near Eastern practice, where such a gesture was used before gods *(Fyre, R.N.: 1972, p. 104)*. As for the chief personage who is being celebrated, he recalls to me the description of Torquemada that the chief of the people who came from the north via Panuco as having a fair and ruddy complexion and sporting a beard *(Bancroft, H.H.: 1883, p. 258)*. Also his rugged profile is not unlike one of the Semitic captives of Rameses III *(University of Chicago: 1963, pl. 599)*.

21

The next question is—could there have been Jews among the Semites? Here a passage in the *Popol Vuh* (5701f.) is relevant. It is stated that the ancestors "passed through as though there were no sea . . . the water divided itself . . . and they were able to walk across". Inevitably we think of Moses dividing the waters for the children of Israel to walk across the Red Sea *(Exodus 14, 21-22)*. Indeed another Quiche Maya text *The Lineage of the Lords of Totonicapan* comes to this conclusion, and states categorically that the ancestor touched the sea with his staff which opened up and closed after because they were the sons of Abraham and Jacob. And elsewhere it calls the Quiche ancestors who came from the sunrise "descendants of Israel" *(Popol Vuh: 1971, p. 163n.)* In the latter text the intimacy with the Old Testament clearly implies post-Columbian knowledge, but surely this cannot be the case with the *Popol Vuh* in which all the Old Testament traits which we shall see in a moment have a thoroughly Maya outlook. Meanwhile, I would like to point out that the miracle performed by Moses and alluded to by the Maya texts was long a familiar one in ancient Egypt. There is thus the tale in which the god Ra foils a pursuit by opening up a great stretch of water between two brothers to separate them *(Erman, A.: 1966, pp. 153-4)*, and the story of the magician of King Sneferu who stacks the water of the lake one on the other simply to retrieve the pendant of a harem girl, and thereafter restores the waters of the lake back to its place *(Erman, A.: 1966, pp. 38-40)*.

Cyrus Gordon *(1971: pp. 154-169)* has shown a whole spate of parallels between the *Popol Vuh* and the *Book of Genesis*. These include creation by fiat, the first man a failure, the first man destroyed by a flood, the survival of some, the clouding of man's sight so he should not have the same vision as god, the creation of woman while the man slept, and lastly the woman reflects on the possibility of death should she eat a wondrous fruit.

Traditionally the *Book of Genesis* is said to have been written by Moses who had fled Egypt not long before the Ramessid expedition. But whether the *Popol Vuh* received the Hebrew Creation account then or very much later is at present not possible to verify. In view of this uncertainty it is not justified to scorn the 19th Century view that the Lost Tribes of Israel had found their way to America. They had escaped from captivity in Assyria under Shalmaneser, and had journeyed for a year and a half till they came to a land where they settled called Arsareth *(Apocryphal Book of Esdras, Bk.4; see further Bancroft, H.H.: 1875, V, p. 78f.)*.

Babylonians

While there are no visible traces of the Canaanites, Phoenicians or Hebrews in Formative Mesoamerica, the case is very different for the Babylonians, as I shall now establish for the first time.

I shall begin by showing that the Babylonian account of the Creation and Destruction of the world and also its chief Epic were known in Mexico and are embedded in its literature. Here are some themes that stem from the Babylonian creation story, the *Enuma Elish*.

1. The *Histoyre du Mechique* preserves the myth of the earth and heaven being formed from the split halves of the earth monster in the primaeval waters *(Nicholson, H.B.: 1971, p. 400)*, which has an amazingly exact parallel *(Pritchard, J.B.: 1955, pp. 66-7, esp. lines 137-8)*.

2. The *Popol Vuh (1971, l. 130f, 432f.)* describes how in the beginning was darkness and the Sea, till the male and female creator gods mated and produced man to provide nourishment and support (for the gods). In the Accadian myth there was first the primordial ocean, then pairs of gods were created, and in turn one of them created man to serve the gods "so they shall be at ease" *(Pritchard, J.B.: 1955, p. 68)*. Thus identical reasons are given for the creation of man.

3. The *Legenda de los Soles* preserves the mode of the creation of man through the blood of the chosen god *(Nicholson, H.B.: 1971, p. 400)* which is once again identical *(Pritchard, J.B.: 1955, p. 68)*.

And the same precise parallels are found for the destruction of man.

1. The reason given for the destruction in the *Popol Vuh* is the same as the Babylonian, that is they made too much noise *(Gordon, C.: 1971, p. 154f.)*.

2. The Mexican myth of the four destructions of mankind was that each was destroyed at the end of a span of time, and the last was drowned in a flood *(Soustelle, J.: 1968, p. 109)*. We now know from an Old Babylonian tablet that according to their belief there were three destructions of mankind, each after a fixed span of time, and the last effected by the Great Flood *(Lambert, W.G. and Millard, A.R.: 1969)*.

3. The Mexican myth in the *Legenda de los Soles* tells of a single couple surviving after the deluge destroyed mankind *(Nicholson, H.B.: 1971, p. 400)*. This must be drawn from the Accadian myth which has a long passage about the surviving couple *(Pritchard, J.B.: 1955, p. 95)*, whereas its counterpart in the Old Testament has the emphasis on the family of Noah.

The Babylonian Flood myth is incorporated in the Gilgamesh legend, and I shall now show that this great Epic was known in Mexico, and its chief protagonists were present there. If I shall have proved this, it would seem as though this was the only story which girdled the globe in antiquity since I have also traced a part of it in India *(Jairazbhoy, R.A.: 1963, pp. 5, 34)*.

1. Enkidu. This is the theme of beguiling the alien man by feminine charm, and in both cases the place where this is enacted is the same. The *Popol Vuh (6515f.)* describes how two beautiful maidens were

sent to the river where the ancestors bathed, and told to undress themselves before them: "And if they desire you, you are to invite them . . . really give yourselves to them". The prototype is the famous passage in *The Gilgamesh Epic* in which a pleasure girl is sent to the watering place and told to take off her clothes there. She was instructed that she should let Enkidu possess her, and that she should welcome his ardour (*Pritchard, 1955: p. 74-5*).

2.   Humbaba, the opponent of Enkidu and Gilgamesh is also called Huwawa (the former being the Old Babylonian version of the name). The name Huwawa is almost identical to the Mexican god Huehue. Huehue is the god of fire; and similarly the text says of Huwawa that —"his mouth is fire"*(Pritchard, J.B.: 1955, p. 78)*. Moreover the facial features of both are formed by means of raised lines of clay *(cf. Easby, E.K.: 1966, fig. 190, p. 39; and Van Buren: 1930, fig. 271, p. 219)*, as Von Wuthenau *(1974, see chart)* has also observed. This Babylonian type was shown to have been diffused westward by the Phoenicians *(Barnett, R.D.: 1960, pp. 147-8)*.

3.   Gilgamesh.   About ¾ mile inside the cave of Juxtlahuaca, in the province of Guerrero, was discovered a painting on the wall in July 1966 *(Coe, M.D.: 1968a, p. 101)*. Since there is an artificial canal 250 feet long going into this part of the cave, and there is also a great plumed snake, it would not be unreasonable to imagine this place as some kind of Underworld shrine. Compare, for example, the relief at Medinet Habu in which Rameses III enters a room representing the Underworld *(University of Chicago: 1941, III, pt. 1, p. 17, fig. 9)*. In Egyptian symbolism you also have a heavenly river called Cool Water *(Erman, A.: 1966, p.8)*, and a primeval serpent which came into being in the dark waters of the Abyss *(Clark, R.T.R.: 1959, p. 51 — Coffin texts)*. Later inscriptions abound in references to "the serpent in the Primeval Darkness" *(Ibid, p. 50)*. In the *Book of the Dead (ch. 87)* there is a serpent who says: "I am Sito who dwells in the farthest regions of the world". Sito is a serpent who encircles the world *(Ibid, pp. 239-40)*. The serpent in the Mexican cave has a crest, and on the centre of its head is an Olmec cross *(Gay, Carlo, T.E.: 1967, p. 34)*.

With the exception of the Oxtotitlan cave, discovered in 1968 *(Grove, D.C.: 1970)*, we have no other surviving wall paintings in the Americas for nearly half a millennium. In the Juxtlahuaca cave a giant-sized figure wearing the skin of a mountain lion stretches out a snake-like instrument in one hand, and a plant-like object in the other towards the small figure of a bearded person before him (Ill. 11).

In Egypt there were deep galleries cut in the rocks and decorated with paintings, but the nearest resemblance to the scene itself is in the Egyptian *Book of the Dead (Budge, E.A.W.: 1913, I, Vignette 15)*, where a priest extends a snake-headed instrument "to open the mouth" of the dead Ani (Ill. 12). He, too, wears a leopard's skin. In both cases the tail of the beast falls between the legs. But here the priest and the deceased are

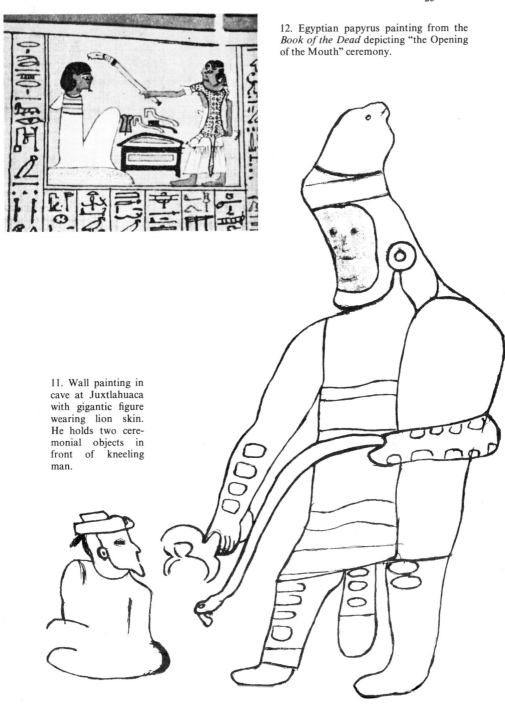

12. Egyptian papyrus painting from the *Book of the Dead* depicting "the Opening of the Mouth" ceremony.

11. Wall painting in cave at Juxtlahuaca with gigantic figure wearing lion skin. He holds two ceremonial objects in front of kneeling man.

exactly the same size. There is a possible explanation if we assume that this is a deified Gilgamesh who initiates the dead into the next world. In Babylonian myth Gilgamesh did not succeed in achieving immortality, but in Sumerian myth he did become the Judge of the Underworld, and to him King Ur Nammu came to be initiated after dying *(Kramer, S.N.: 1969, pp. 111, 119)*. Besides Gilgamesh was imagined as having a height of 16 feet *(Saggs, H.W.F.: 1965, p. 87)*. In the Babylonian myth Gilgamesh wore his lion skin, and went to the far West of the World across difficult seas and in one place passing through a mountain in thick darkness. All these events in the life of Gilgamesh, his description, and his eventual Underworld role, serve to identify the personage at Juxtlahuaca. Gilgamesh had come to the West in search of the Plant of Life, and as I see it, here he is proffering it to the deceased with one hand while opening its mouth with the other in an Egyptian ceremony for which I shall show Mexican evidence below (see p. 79).   If the Juxtlahuaca painting was executed under the direction of a Babylonian priest he would have had no difficulty in reconciling with the Egyptian cult practice, since the Babylonians themselves had a rite of "washing and opening the mouth" of statues, and it took place on the river, and like that of Egypt the rite was celebrated at dawn *(Blackman, A.M.: 1924, p. 47f)*. It could be that there were two possible survivals of all this in later native memory. One is the Tzendal tradition that their culture hero Votan penetrated into the Underworld through a cave *(Brinton, D.C.: 1882)*, and the other is that the name of Gilgamesh survives in Gucumatz, the creator god of the Quiche Maya.

The representation of Gilgamesh is not the only visible sign of the Babylonian presence. Most conspicuously of course there is the ziggurat on which the Mexican stepped temple is based. We shall investigate this whole question in an Appendix (p. 114 f.). Possibly also the use of plano-convex adobe bricks in an Olmecoid context of c. 850 B.C. in Oaxaca *(Flannery, K.V.: 1966-69, pp. 30, 32)* can be attributed to Mesopotamian mediation, and the contemporary use of iron ore for mirrors in the same region *(ibid, p. 108f.)* is suggestive of Iron Age activities in the Old World of that time.

And now finally I shall show the presence of a Babylonian goddess about 100 miles north of the site of the Cave, at a place called Chalcatzingo. One of the reliefs here, high on a cliff face overlooking agricultural lands, represents a goddess seated in the mouth of a shallow cave (ill. 13) *(Coe, M.D.: 1968a, p. 93)*. She holds a large tablet in her lap. Smoke spirals in front of her. Outside, large drops of rain fall, and great clumps of corn grow. This description exactly fits the goddess of grain Nisaba. She too carried a tablet, and Gudea who dreamed of her, and wanted to know who she was, was told her name and that what she carried was "the tablet of the favourable star of heaven" *(Barton, G.A.: 1929, pp. 205-13)*. This Sumerian hymn to Nisaba translated recently *(Hallo, W.W.: 1970, pp. 116-34)* seems to describe the goddess of Chalcatzingo with uncanny accuracy:

Rock relief at Chalcatzingo with ▪uds and rain and vegetation sprouting and goddess seated in mouth of cave, ▪ntified as the Babylonian goddess ▪aba.

"O Lady coloured like the stars of heaven
Holding (on her lap) the lapis lazuli tablet,
Nisaba born in the great sheep fold by the divine Earth...
Mouth-opened by the seven flutes,
Dragon, emerging brightly on the festival,
Mother-goddess of the nation...
Pacifying the habitat with cold water,
Providing the foreign mountain-land with plenty...
In order to make grain and vegetable grow in the furrow,
So that the excellent corn can be marvelled at ...
In the *Abzu* of Eridu sanctuaries are apportioned,
Nisaba, woman born in the mountain."

Although a Sumerian goddess, statues to Nisaba date from after the 2nd millennium B.C. *(Spycket, A.: 1968),* a fact which at once eliminates the time gap.

There is only one element at Chalcatzingo which appears to be extraneous, and that is the solar symbol resting like an eye on top of the cave. The flattened disc of the sun shows that it is sinking into the horizon; the typically Olmec X across it may describe the Underworld sun, a conception which is peculiarly Mexican and initially Egyptian (see p.67).

27

PART 3

Institutions and Customs

Monarchy

It is assumed that the institution of monarchy was universal in ancient times. But the fact is that it was contrived by man, and hence could have been diffused from place to place. One evidence of this is the Sumerian myth which relates how a number of institutions and skills were transmitted from the city of Eridu by boat up river, and among these was a knowledge of the functions of kings *(Jairazbhoy, R.A.: 1963, p. 10)*. And again the Maya Epic the *Popol Vuh* (7240f.) describes how their ancestors came across the seas from the sunrise, and brought with them among other things the insignia of lordship, including the canopy and throne. I have detected a strong pointer to kingship having come from Egypt, though it survives in a non-Maya area. The ritual is described in a Nahua poem in which the initiate turns to the four quarters, hurls his arrow in each, and attains to the gods *(Nicholson, I.: 1968, p. 22)*. So in the Egyptian Sed Festival the Pharaoh faced the cardinal points, shot an arrow in each point, and was proclaimed *(Frankfort, H.: 1948, p. 79f; Fairman, H.W.: 1958, pp. 83-4)*.

More than this there are pointers to divine kingship having been introduced in Olmec times. In a text from the year 12 at Medinat Habu the god Ptah-Tatenen says to the king that he assumed his form as the Ram, and cohabited with Rameses's mother in order to fashion him *(Edgerton, W.F. and Wilson, J.A.: 1936, pp. 120-1)*. The implication of this is that Rameses was semi-divine. And this theme is encountered in an Olmec sculpture excavated at Potrero Nuevo. Although it is fragmentary it is clear that a jaguar is mating with a woman who lies on her back (Ill. 14) *(Stirling, M.W.: 1955, pp. 19-20; pls. 25, 26a)*. How can we be

14. Conjectural sketch of Olmec sculpture from Potrero Nuevo with jaguar copulating with woman. Comparable with ram copulating with the mother of Rameses III.

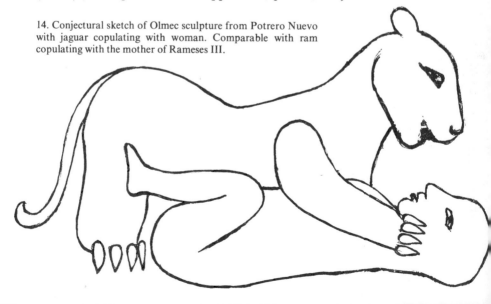

sure that though the *motif* of the animal copulating with a woman is the same in Olmec sculpture and Ramessid texts, the *implications* too are the same, that is they both refer to the royal heir? The answer is that where the same theme recurs in a later sculpture from San Agustin in Colombia, the Paez Indians who live nearby confirm the belief that the rape of a woman by a jaguar resulted in a thunder child who grew up to be an important culture hero *(Reichel-Dolmatoff, G.: 1972, p. 51f).*

Another possible trace of Egyptian royalty in Olmec times is the use of a double crown. The Olmec dignitary carved on a quadrangular pillar (Ill. 15) raises up one hand as if to support his headdress which consists of two animals one above the other. One is a falcon and the other is non-descript. The double crown (symbolising the two parts of the country) is an exclusively Egyptian conception, and it is usual for the king to wear a serpent symbol over his brow and the Queen to wear a vulture *(Posener, G.: 1962, pp. 213, 235)* though here they are combined. The Olmec "king" is conferring what appears to be a contained cross to the seated negroid person before him. If this glyph means "the underworld sun", then he could be saying what a god says to a queen in a Ramessid tomb: "I give to thee a place in the Sacred Land" *(Thausing and Goedicke, H.: 1971, p. 52).* This is paralleled by the wish in an Aztec poem "May I be sent to the House of the Sun" *(Hawkes, J.: 1962, p. 148).*

15. Olmec pillar with relief of dignitary with double-crown proffering glyph with cross (?) to seated negroid figure. (Museo Nacional, Mexico City).

Slavery

It could be that the Egyptians introduced the idea of slavery on a grand scale in the New World. Certainly the massive Olmec monuments and ceremonial centres imply a vast organisation of labour scarcely known in the Americas before that time.

An evidence of the introduction of slavery may be the flat stamps *(sellos)* that first appear in Olmec culture. These are thought to have been possibly used for body decoration. If so this may have been suggested by the branding on the bodies of slaves. In Egypt slaves had been branded with the cartouche of Rameses III *(Edgerton, W.F. and Wilson, J.A.: 1936, p. 27)*. While in Mesopotamia the slavery mark was on the forehead *(Pritchard, J.B.: 1955, p. 437)*, we know that Egyptians branded the Sea Peoples on the shoulder *(Edgerton and Wilson, 1936, p. 42)*. A relief at Medinat Habu shows officers branding Philistine prisoners on the shoulder while the long handles of branding tools project from the brazier on the ground *(Nelson, H.H. and Hoelscher, U.: 1929, pp. 34-5, fig. 25)*. The practice appears to have originated at least as early as Rameses II's statues which had his names cut upon the shoulders or down the back *(British Museum: 1909, pp. 160, 161, nos. 576, 584)*. It may not be just chance that the stamp decoration on an Olmec clay figurine runs down the back from the shoulder *(Field, F.V.: 1967, fig. 7, p. 12)*.

A girl on the side of an Olmec monolith appears to be a slave (Ill. 16), for she is tied by a rope which is held by her master who is depicted on the front (Ill. 83). The relationship is the same in which the Egyptian king is represented holding his captive enemies by a rope, and they are depicted on the side of this throne *(Davies, N.M.: 1936, pl. xxix; cf. Winlock, H.E.: 1942, p. 12)*. The reason for their being tied in this way is explained by a Ramessid text which says that it was to prevent them running away *(Montet, P.: 1958, p. 63)*. The girl on the Olmec monolith is likely to be a concubine, for even in later times some Aztec kings were born of slave girls *(Bray, W.: 1968, p. 81)*.

There is one story told in the *Popol Vuh* (6765f.) which not only has Egyptian parallels, but ends on the same note in slavery. The tribes besiege a shrine area, open up jars of wasps in the town, and take captives telling them "you will be servants". So in the Egyptian story "the Siege of Joppa" baskets with soldiers hidden in them are taken into the besieged city, they emerge and capture the city, and put the inhabitants into bonds and fetters and make them into slaves *(Pritchard: 1955, pp. 22-3; Erman: 1966, pp. 167-9)*.

Dwarfs

It could be that the Egyptians introduced the cult of the dwarf, for there was such a cult in ancient Egypt. They were depicted with crooked legs and arms, and some represented the creator god Ptah *(Holmberg, M.S.: 1946,*

16. Olmec relief of slave woman tied with rope held in the hand of her master. (see Ill. 83).

pp. 182-3). A hollow pottery figurine from the Tehuacan valley seems to be a dwarf; the excavators admit that it resembles Egyptian figures in "the large almond-shaped eyes" *(MacNeish et al: 1970, pp. 53-55).* I would add that the strip going vertically over the crown is like that on the helmet of Rameses II *(Hayes, W.C.: 1959, p. 342, fig. 216).* According to Motolinia, Montezuma had in his palace dwarfs and little hunchbacks who were purposely deformed as children *(Motolinia: 1950, p. 212).* He calls them servants but Bernal Diaz says they were jesters *(1963, p. 227).*

Customs

To point to traditional practices uniquely common to Egypt and Mexico is no mean task. In the case of sexual customs this is just possible. One cannot always be certain that the practice was not prevalent elsewhere, even though no other evidence survives to show this. Take the case of aphrodisiacs. We have no certain indication that their use was widespread in antiquity. But we do know that it was ritually used in Egypt in the form of the white sap of the cos lettuce which was believed to have aphrodisiac qualities *(Posener, G.: 1962, p. 171).* On the occasion of opening the harvest season, stumps of cos lettuce were ceremonially offered to the

31

17. Olmecoid reliefs from Monte Alban popularly called "Los Danzantes", but actually prisoners with penises cut off. Notice figure on top left of man holding instrument (now Museo Nacional, Mexico City).

fertility god Min, as in one instance Rameses III is doing *(University of Chicago: 1953, pls. 428, 444).* In late Maya times the *plumeria* flower served as a love charm, and was condemned c.1320 for spreading excessive adultery in the land *(Tozzer, A.M.: 1957, I, p. 47; see p. 111 also).* If one day it will become possible to demonstrate the use of aphrodisiacs in Olmec times, then the probability of transmission from Egypt will gain added strength. Meanwhile, we can give further support to this idea by referring to the other sexual innovations brought from Egypt including the copulating god (see above p. 28), the agricultural fertility procession and the phallic mutilation (see below pp.46-7), and two other practices— circumcision and penis truncation, which we shall now investigate in some detail.

Circumcision is a practice so typical of the Semites that it is often forgotten that it was a very old custom in Egypt too, though evidently performed at puberty. Indeed there is even a representation of a young boy standing and having his foreskin operated without much fuss *(Posener, G.: 1962, p. 46).* It comes as a surprise to learn that the Totonacs of Mexico practiced circumcision. It was necessary for every male child by the age of one month *(Tuggle, H.D.: 1968, p. 68).* There were

other places in America where the custom prevailed *(Loeb, E.: 1923, pp. 18-19, 35)*, but it is quite uncertain how old the practice was in these areas.

Another Egyptian custom is so exclusive to itself that in my estimation there can be not the slightest doubt of Egyptian presence in Mexico. When Rameses III took all the Lybian warriors captive after defeating the Sea Peoples, he had their male organs cut off. They were thrown in a heap and counted by scribes *(Montet, P.: 1958, p. 246)*. Heaps of phalli are actually represented in the Medinat Habu reliefs *(University of Chicago: 1932, I, pls. 22, 23; II, pl. 75)*. An inscription gives the totals of two piles of phalli of the Lybians as 12,535 and 12,860 *(Edgerton, W.F. and Wilson, J.A.: 1936, pp. 13-14)*. It could be that this was not done simply for taking a convenient census, but to ensure that there would be no further issue and one day their sons may not once again invade Egypt. This is exactly what happened when, according to the myth, Seth lost his testicles in his fight with Horus previously. He was mocked because now he could not bear issue; to use the words of the text "his seed will be destroyed" *(Clark, R.T.R.: 1959, p. 210)*. Now if we look closely at the Olmecoid reliefs at Monte Alban (Ill. 17), we shall see that the men depicted here have had their penises truncated, and blood flows from their wound. It is customary to call them *los danzantes,* the dancers, because of their curious gestures of their arms and legs. But now this description will have to be given up in favour of my view that they are limp, grimacing, some even cringing, and are very much dead. Even in the Olmec area itself, there are representations of jaguar warriors, holding aloft the virile member as a trophy of war, just as the American Indian later held scalps. In the other hand of the warrior there is a deadly instrument for the operation, though in my view the character of both objects has been misconstrued hitherto *(Antonieta Cervantes, M.: 1969, p.37f.)* and on one example which was omitted from the series reviewed *(Metropolitan Museum of Art: 1970, fig. 37),* the identification is quite unmistakeable. And again the "danzante" slabs on view in the Museo Nacional show a miniature figure holding one of these dissecting instruments just above a victim whose thighs are discoloured with still-surviving red paint. In the Jalapa Museum there is a monumental sculpture of such an executioner-priest with ritual instrument, and within it a faint imprint of the truncated organ (Ill. 18). From the Monte Alban reliefs I would conclude that the Olmecs invaded this part of South Central Mexico, mutilated their victims to bring an end to their progeny in the manner to which they had once been accustomed, and set up these as a record or tally.

18. Priest wearing jaguar mask with instrument in hands identified here as penis-truncator. (Jalapa Museum).

* This is not to deny that some of them have ceremonial celts in their hands as emblems of authority (e.g. a celt found in a sarcophagus at La Venta was as though held in the corpse's hand — Covarrubias, M.: n.d., p. 93). However the origin and implication of the jade celt held in the hand is elucidated below (see p. 106).

PART 4

Art and Culture

Art

Monumental architecture, sculpture and painting may all have been introduced into Mexico by the Egyptian migrants. There are direct and indirect reasons for believing this to have been the case. The direct reason is that apparently none of these traits appear prior to the 12th Century B.C., and then suddenly they all appear fully formed. The indirect reason is that in all their earlier manifestations there are explicit links with the Old World. In architecture the stepped temple is related to the Babylonian ziggurat (see below p.118f), in painting the earliest surviving example at Juxtlahuaca is portraying an Egypto-Babylonian theme (see above p.26), and in sculpture the monumental negroid heads continue a Pharaonic practice of colossal sculpture in carving and transporting (see above p.19). To add to this, relief sculpture also displays Old World kinship. In the relief of the 'Semite' who is being celebrated (see p. 21) it is admitted that there are two ways in which they are related to Egyptian and Assyrian styles. Firstly the minor figures are portrayed smaller because they are less important, and secondly the persons farther away are situated above which results in a kind of aerial perspective, whether this was deliberate or not *(Heizer, R.F.: 1967, pp. 35-6)*. Besides, several Olmec sculptures and reliefs have been explained in the course of this book in terms of Old World symbolism. As for the lesser arts, it appears that finger rings, and cylindrical stamps (Ill. 19) equivalent to the Mesopotamian cylinder seals, first appear in Mesoamerica c.1200 B.C. *(Ford, J.A.: 1969, p. 84)*, like so many other things. Where cylinder seals appear outside the Babylonian area in the Old World, no one doubts their ultimate source, and there is no reason for treating Mesoamerica as an exception.

19. Olmec cylindrical seal with signs for marking body or goods. Comparable to Babylonian cylinder seals, though larger.

There are also some special types of terracotta animals. Among these is a turtle with movable head from the Museum at Villahermosa (Ill. 20). For this too we have Egyptian prototypes not only in the many movable toys such as the crocodile with movable jaw *(Wilkinson, J.G.: 1980, I, p. 197)*, but also a turtle on a magical rod which had holes intended for wooden tenons *(Fischer, H.G.: 1968, pl. 19, pp. 32-3)*. Other such activated Egyptian toys now on display at the British Museum from c.1300 B.C. include a lion with movable tongue, and a mouse with movable jaw and tail *(British Museum, Acc. nos. 36117, 65512)*, while a Ramessid dog at the Louvre has a movable jaw *(Musée du Louvre: 1952, pl. XII, 1)*. Movable jaws and tongues are encountered in metal-work of the Mixtec region *(Bray, W.: 1968, p. 130)*. Motolinia tells us that the Indians could cast birds with movable tongues, heads and wings, and monkeys or other beasts which could move their head, hands and feet *(Motolinia: 1950, p. 241)*.

20. Terracotta tortoise with movable head.
Compare with similar Egyptian toys.
(Villahermosa Museum).

One type of zoomorpnic pottery could have been introduced by the Egyptian immigrants. The black polished duck from Tlatilco *(Feuchtwanger, F.: 1955, pl. 11)* should be compared with the black pottery duck from Egypt, though this is of rather earlier date c.1600 B.C. *(Kern, J.H.C.: 1961, p.1f.)*.

Culture

Under this heading I have collected a number of traits including music, sport, agriculture, writing and literature.

Music

It is likely that the Egyptians imported the musical instrument called the sistrum into Mesoamerica. One reason for believing this is that while in Egypt the sistrum was sacred to Isis, in Mexico it was the instrument of the corn mother Xilonen *(Sahagun: 1950-63, Bk. 2, p. 99)*, and its use was forbidden except for religious purposes *(Stevenson, R.: 1968, p. 39)*. Moreover it has been observed that the type of sistrum that occurs in Mexico in Yaqui territory is very much like the Abyssinian instrument *(Izikowitz, K.G.: 1970 reprint, p. 151; cf. Marti, S.: 1968, p. 56)*.

Sport

It could be that the Egyptian mercenaries introduced both wrestling and single-stick fighting into Mesoamerica. The only evidence for wrestling is the statue of the well known Olmec with beautifully equipoised arms who is generally regarded as a wrestler (Ill. 21). But while he remains quite isolated in time in the Mesoamerican context, wrestling was such a

21. Olmec sculpture of figure thought to be a wrestler, Museo Nacional, Mexico City.

37

popular sport at the Egyptian court that long snatches of their conversation are recorded *(Murray, M.A.: 1965, p. 115),* and there are numerous paintings depicting the sport. Just below the window of Royal Appearances at Medinet Habu in which Rameses III used to stand overlooking the court are corbelled heads of prisoners, and below these is an audience witnessing contenders wrestling and fighting with the stick *(University of Chicago: 1932, II, pls. 111, 112).*

Clear evidence for the single stick sport does not exist in Mesoamerica, but a memory of it seems to have survived in the Maya dance, the Colomche, in which the dancers painted black struck and parried with reeds and sticks *(Kurath, G.P. and Marti, S.: 1964, p. 28).* As far as single-stick combat is concerned it is not a little curious that what we know of the protection worn by these fighters in the time of Rameses III seems so close to the representations of ball players in Olmecoid art. It is possible that the protective equipment was suggested by the Egyptians, unique as they are in the whole history of sport in the ancient world. I juxtapose a description of the respective gear, and leave it for the reader to form an interim judgement. The Egyptian single-stick fighters had their left forearms strapped up, right hands padded with a leather gauntlet, and chins and cheek protected by a thick bandage attached to a band round their forehead *(Montet, P.: 1958, p. 228).* We also have a representation in which they wear leather helmets over the skull and neck, while pads hang from the waist over the loins *(Touny, A.D.: and Wenig, S.: 1969, pls. 15-18).* Compare these with the figurines of Tlapacoya ball players. Their arms, wrists, knees and ankles have thick protective bands. They also have pads dangling over hips, and wide belts protruding toward the front. Some wear masks over the lower part of the face, while others have padded headdresses *(Coe, M.D.: 1965, p. 54; figs. 100, 151, 152, 157, 158).*

Agriculture

Of course agriculture as such is very ancient in America, but there is no sign that irrigation was practised before the appearance of the Olmecs. And the Olmecs seem to have shared one unique practice with the Egyptians. It was pointed out that they depended on river inundations for corn cultivation *(Caso, A.: 1965, pp. 3f.).*

Writing

Since writing first appears in America under the Olmecs we must question its origin. The hieroglyphs from Olmec times owe almost nothing to Egypt, and have not been deciphered.

And yet a number of reasons lead to the conclusion that hieroglyphic writing did come from Egypt. One is that precisely the type of seated Egyptian scribe is found in Olmec sculpture. Another is that at least two Egyptian hieroglyphs are so far recognisable in Mexico, one of them certainly having the same meaning as in Egypt. We shall see both the scribes and the glyphs in detail in a moment. The third reason for believing that there must have been scribes who brought their writings is that all the Egyptian ideas and conceptions (particularly in connection with gods and the Underworld) are so precise in their equivalent as to almost conform letter by letter. And finally the account that Sahagun gives of the first ancestors who came to this land across the seas tells that they included among them "bookmen". And the reason why the original writing was not preserved also emerges from this account. Sahagun writes that the ancestors arrived at a place called Tamoanchan led by their priests *(1950-63; Bk. 10, p. 190).*

Leaving most of their group there, the wise men called Amoxaque (bookmen) went taking with them their writings, the books, the paintings, the crafts, and the casting of metals. Four wise men remained. They wondered how they could lead and govern, and how they could make a beginning. And then they set about contriving the calendar, and this calendar is the one still in existance. The neglected account of Sahagun clearly tells how the immigrant ancestors went taking their knowledge with them, and the remaining seers reinvented the machinery to prevent the rule from breaking up. This statement is in accord with my view that the calendar and glyphs were reinvented in Mesoamerica after exposure to foreign prototypes once these were no longer available. A time-lag would explain why all memory of the type of writing their forefathers used was erased, and simply the notion that it could be written down by symbols had survived. They had to invent new symbols, and they began with day signs and numerals. We are now able to read the date on stele from the third century B.C. and later. Incidentally comparisons have been made between Egyptian and Aztec numbering *(Guitel, G.: 1958, pp. 52-56),* but there are no striking correspondences that we can point to. Though the bar for numbering could have come from Shang dynasty China.

There is a headless statue from San Lorenzo (Ill. 22) that looks astonishingly like an Egyptian scribe. He has what seems to be a closed scroll in

22. Headless Olmec sculpture holding what could be a scroll. Squatting in the conventional manner of Egyptian scribes. Kilt dress typically ending at knee. (Jalapa Museum).

39

his lap. The manner of his sitting cross-legged with the hem of his kilt going over his knees, his broad-shouldered, straight-backed deportment are closely comparable to seated Egyptian scribes, for example a Theban scribe from the reign of Amenhotep III (Ill. 23) *(Hayes, W.C.: 1959, pt. 2, fig. 160)*. The treatment of the hairstyle of the latter with incised lines going straight back toward the crown resembles another miniature seated jade figure from La Venta (Ill. 24) *(Bernal, I.: 1968, pl. 45a)*, whose kilt is again treated in the same manner. It must have been priests and scribes who were really instrumental in introducing Egyptian ideas and beliefs to America, and one imagines that they had once been attached to the House of Life, as was the case with the scribe sent on an expedition by Rameses IV *(Montet, P.: 1958, p. 298)*. There are two more Olmec works in Villahermosa which indicate that there was literacy although no substantial amount of writing has survived in the Olmec area proper.

23, Seated Egyptian scribe from Thebes with scroll on lap and kilt over knees. (Metropolitan Museum of Art, New York).

24. Olmec priest in jade squatting in identical posture also with kilt over knees. From La Venta. (Museo Nacional, Mexico City).

There is a headless statue from La Venta now in the Museum who holds the edge of a tablet with his left hand and clenches his right hand in an attitude of writing, and there are two depressed lines on the tablet. Then there is a "cavern" scene on a boulder at the Parque La Venta on the side of which is the relief of a scribe seemingly instructing a pupil who is older than himself (Ill. 25). The manner in which he stretches out his hand to the writing hand of his instructor, is reminiscent of the Egyptian boy who is holding out his hand toward the writing hand of his master (Ill. 25a) *(Isha L.S. de: 1954, p. 108),* and needless to say there are no contemporary representations of the sort anywhere. This leads to the hope that one day Egyptian hieroglyphic texts may turn up in the Gulf area.

25. Olmec relief at Parque La Venta, Villahermosa, with scribe instructing pupil who is seated at lower level.

25a. Egyptian scribe teaching pupil. Thebes c.1420 B.C. Same profile view, same theme, and same gesture as Olmec sculpture.

One Egyptian hieroglyphic symbol has already been identified on a cylinder seal from Chiapa de Corzo; it is a triangle partly bisected at the base *(Kelley, D.H.: 1966, pp. 744-5)*. Another Egyptian hieroglyph is used monumentally, and I now identify it here. The little Olmec atlantes on a carved altar from Potrero Nuovo (see Ill. 41) support with their hands conventionalised symbols exactly identical to the Egyptian hieroglyph for the "sky" *(Gardiner, A.H.: 1927, p. 474)*. There is for example an uplifted sky sign on a relief of Ramessid date *(Helck, W.: 1968, II, pl. 27)*. Moreover the sky goddess Nut herself supports the sky symbol in coffins (see Ill. 42) *(Neugebauer, O. and Parker, R.A.: 1960, I, pl. 4)* precisely in this manner.

Literature

Kroeber claimed that the American Indians remained proverbless because the habit was never transmitted to them from the Old World where both primitive and advanced peoples used it *(Kroeber, A.L.: 1948, p. 544)*. He seems not to have been aware of those collected by Sahagun in Mexico, who prefaces them with the comment "Here are told some of the sayings called adages which they told and (still) tell" *(Sahagun: 1950-69, Bk. 6, p. 219f; Bk. 1, pp. 81-4)*. The example that he gives of solar phases which end with the soul's convergence with the sun is derived from Egyptian myth, as I have shown (see p. 11). The general absence of proverbs in the New World and an ancient Oriental theme in the few that do occur, are together indications that they were introduced by the Egypto-Olmec migrants.

PART 5
Rituals

The religious rituals to be discussed below undoubtedly exist elsewhere, but on account of the unique impress that they took in Egypt and Mexico, it can be shown that they were almost certainly transmitted. It is only the fact of very recent excavation and discovery that enables us to arrive at such a positive conclusion. The three rituals investigated here are libations, incense and the phallic cult. All of these are now attested in the Olmec period.

Libations

In the Parque La Venta at Villahermosa is the Olmec sculpture of a short kneeling man (Ill. 26). He holds an object in his hands which appears to be a stone trough. This posture is typically Egyptian in which the object held is either an offering table, such as Rameses II holds on a sculpture from Abydos *(British Museum No. 96),* or libation basins as this Olmec sculpture seems to represent.

26. Olmec sculpture (Villahermosa) with kneeling figure holding basin possibly signifying libation in the Egyptian manner.

43

Fortunately another libation ceremony survives in Mexico which proves conclusively its Egyptian ancestry. It was already illustrated and pointed out by Chavero in 1887 *(Riva Palacio, D.V.: 1887, I, p. 233)*. The manner in which the Underworld gods Mictlantecuhtli and his consort pour crossed libation streams from vases over the head of another god in *Codex Borgia (Seler, E.: 1906, II, pl. 31)*, is identical to a pair of Egyptian gods pouring crossed libation streams from vases over the Pharaoh's head (Ills. 27, 28). It is significant that there are at least three representations of Rameses III being purified by the water of life in this fashion *(Gardiner, A.: 1950, p. 3f.)*. We can perhaps link this with the practice of the lords of Chalco who preserved the body by desiccation. They made libations by pouring water on the mummy's head. They did this saying "this is the water which thou usedst in this world" *(Bancroft, H.H.: 1875, II, pp.603-4)*. It seems to me that this is comparable with the *Pyramid Text* in which libations were poured out before the statue of the mummy to restore to it the moisture which the body had in life *(Blackman, A.M.: Bd. 50, cited by Elliot Smith, G.: 1929, p. 42)*.

27. Egyptian libation scene with Pharaoh purified by the gods Thoth and Horus. Notice crossed streams.

28. Scene from Mexican Codex with crossed streams of libation poured by two Underworld gods over another.

Incense

In the case of incense it can be shown that the type of ritual implement, the actual form, the manner of using the incense and its very name in Mesoamerica, can be traced back to Egypt. The censer as a spoon with long handle is common to both areas, and what is more in both areas some

29. A Mexican cen-
ser in the form of
stem with bowl and
animal   terminal
(Seler).

examples have zoomorphic terminations which are upside down (Ill. 29),
(Seler, E.: 1902, II, Abb. 3, p. 292). Here is another remarkable parallel.
Rameses III is shown throwing pellets of incense into the bowl which he
holds in one hand (Ill. 30) *(University of Chicago: 1963, V, pl. 288),* and
in just this manner a priest in *Codex Selden* throws lumps of incense into
the bowl of the incense spoon which he holds in his hand (Ill. 31) *(Caso, A.:
1964, unnumbered).* The censer-spoon can now be shown in the Olmec
context since bowls with tubes have been found in the new Olmec site at
Xochipala in Guerrero *(Furst, P.T.: 1972, p. 352).* And again the Mexican
name for incense, *copal,* does resemble the Egyptian name for incense
mixture, *kuphi,* as Plutarch gives it *(Wilkinson, J.G.: 1890, I, p. 265),*
or *kp* for "censer" in the Egyptian texts *(Gardiner, J.G.: 1950, p. 530).* In
Mexico *copal* was used in the form of balls, and so also in Egypt balls of
incense were used in religious rituals *(David, A. Rosalie: 1973, p. 119).*
After all the *Popol Vuh* (5921-2) does admit that the ancestors who were
the first to come across the sea from the sunrise "untied the incense they
had brought from there". And finally it is notable that the manner in

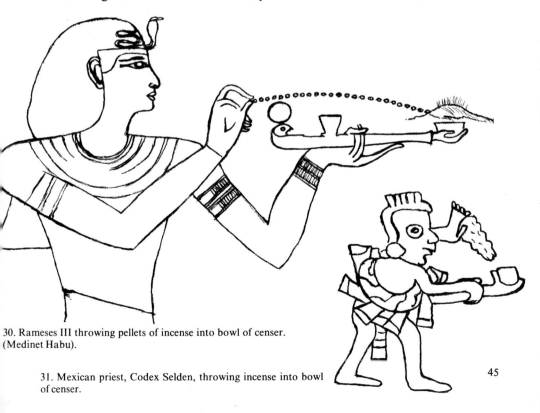

30. Rameses III throwing pellets of incense into bowl of censer.
(Medinet Habu).

31. Mexican priest, Codex Selden, throwing incense into bowl
of censer.

45

which Rameses III holds a round pot in each hand as offering (Ill. 33) *(University of Chicago, V, pls. 265, 295)* is identical with some of the gods in the form of effigy incense burners from Mayapan (Ill. 33) *(Thompson, J.E.S.: 1957, p. 631, figs. 3a and 3f)*. Even though this is a late object, somewhere through a missing link it could be tied up with its Egyptian prototype.

32. Incense burner from Mayapan with priest holding round balls of incense in both hands.

33. Egyptian Pharaoh offering wine or ointment in round bowls with both hands.

The Phallic Cult

Chalcatzingo, where we had encountered the rain and fertility goddess (Ill.13), must have become a center for agricultural ritual. Another relief there is equally fascinating. One jaguar masked man moving to the left holds a corn plant, and the two others moving right hold boat paddles erect (Ill. 34). In this respect they recall the sailors of Ra standing in file each with a paddle in his hands in the Egyptian *Book of the Underworld (Budge, E.A.W.: 1906, I, p. 189)*. In front of them lying down is another jaguar man divested of his mask and clothes with his nakedness revealed. The scene is suggested to be a ceremony of fecundity *(Bernal, I.: 1968, p. 187, pl. 77)*. The implication must be that the goddess of fertility is sexually stimulated, and hence the crops thrive. This is, as far as we know,

34. Olmec relief at Chalcatzingo with procession of jaguar men approaching phallic figure in fertility cult.

35. Phallic procession in Mexican Codex Borbonicus holding artificial phalluses.

the first appearance of the phallic cult in the Americas, and we may legitimately ask whether it was a custom brought over by these new immigrants. This is not the place to go into all the phallic cults known in which to use the phrase of St. Augustine, "the god had to be placated for the success of the crops", but it was prevalent in other places around the Mediterranean as well. The phallus was carried in procession in village fertility rites in Italy *(St. Augustine: Civitas Dei, VII, 21)* in Greece *(Cornford, F.M.: 1934, pp. 48, 50-51)*, and in Egypt, and in fact Herodotus (II. 49) claims that the cult was introduced into Greece from Egypt by Melampus with slight changes. He describes the Egyptian festival in which cubit long phallic images manipulated by strings were carried by women in procession round the villages. On a relief of Rameses III at Medinet Habu a life-sized statue of the phallic god Min is carried in the arms of a priest, while procession bearers hold staffs with phalli (?) dangling from them *(cf. Gauthier, H.: 1931, pls. XII, XIV, p. 277)*. Another relief at Luxor has the phallic god borne on a litter. A rectangular veil or screen covers the bodies of the litter bearers *(Gayet, al: 1894, pl. LIV, fig. 129)*. This surely suggests that they are naked, which recalls the naked man in the procession at Chalcatzingo. And in any case in Egypt likewise Osiris lies on his back with erect phallus *(Rosellini, I.: 1844, III, pl. XXIII)*.

Careful search reveals every detail of the Egyptian phallic cult in Mexico. In 1969 the Museum of Villahermosa acquired an Olmec phallus with a human head: it was almost exactly a cubit in length, an Egyptian cubit being 20.6 inches. Secondly, an Aztec festival had a phallic procession connected with it *(Margain Araujo, C.R.: 1945, pp. 157-74)*, and in *Codex Borbonicus* we can see the Huastec servants with huge artificial phalluses (Ill. 35) moving toward the goddess Teteo innan (Mother of the Gods), a goddess especially venerated on the Vera Cruz

47

coast. This is stated to have taken place at the end of the rainy season at harvest time *(Seler, E.: 1902-03, p. 100)*. Finally the practice of tying the member with a string in ritual survives among the Mayas; Landa says they performed a ceremonial dance thus *(Von Hagen, V.W.: 1960, pp. 138-9)*.

The sculptured figures from Telantunich in Yucatan who hold their phalluses are admitted to be negroid *(Andrews, E.W.: 1939, p. 78, pl. 1e)*. Similarly there are terracotta figurines in Peruvian collections *(Feriz, H.: 1966, pp. 173-81)* and in Mexico in the Museum of Diego Rivera who hold their erect phalluses (Ill.36). So did the Egyptian god Min, sometimes more discreetly under his robe, but occasionally quite openly as on a bronze from Medinet Habu (Ill. 37) *(Daressy, G. 1906, no. 38479)*. Another feature of Min is that he holds one hand bent at the elbow and pointing up. Again an Olmec figure painted in the Cave at Oxtotitlan, Guerrero, displays his phallus and upraises one arm bent at the elbow (Ill. 38) *(Grove, D.C.: 1970)*. And in 1969 there was found on the summit of the hill at Chalcatzingo, a relief of the head of a goggle-eyed man with one hand extended above *(Gay, Carlo, T.E.: 1971, pp. 66-9)*. The Olmec negroes must have made the head of the rain-god in their own guise. In other respects he must have played the role of Min who was also conceived as a rain god "opening the clouds" and giving life to the vegetation *(James, E.O.: 1958, p. 52)*.

The rain falling in the relief of the agricultural goddess at Chalcatzingo (Ill. 13) has been shown to be in the form of little phalluses by analogy with little phallic figures from Tlatilco *(Salas, Lorenzo Ochoa: 1973, p. 123f)*. I conclude from the message of this relief, its neighbouring one, and the raingod at the summit, that at Chalcatzingo the Egyptian and Babylonian priests had pooled their resources in an endeavour to bring abundance to the land.

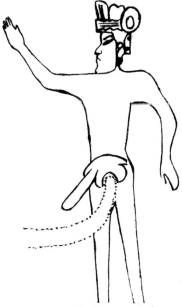

38. Olmec painting of phallic figure from Oxtotitlan with right arm upraised.

37. Egyptian God Min from Medinet Habu holding phallus and raising right hand.

36. Mexican terracotta figurine with m holding phallus in the manner of Egyptian god Min (Museum of Die Rivera, Mexico City).

PART 6
Egyptian Gods in Mexico

I propose now to identify over twenty Egyptian gods in Pre-Columbian Mexico. About half the gods I shall deal with are found already in the Olmec context. The remainder appear visually or in texts of later times, and I claim that they are survivals whose earlier counterparts may appear in due course. Of the first category the most distinctive god to my mind is — *God 1* — Aken. This outlandish creature, which by the way is perfectly human from the back, is now in the Jalapa Museum (Ill. 39). A pair of ropes hang from his mouth. A text from *The Book of Gates* in the Tomb of Rameses VI says: "The double rope comes out of the mouth of Aken: when the twisted one comes out the hour is born . . . then Aken swallows the double rope" *(Piankoff, A.: 1954, p. 174).* He is in other words like an hourglass counting out the 12 hours of the night in the Underworld. Aken is not given monumental status in Egypt, but he is pictorially conceived in this same Tomb of Rameses VI with a double-looped rope attached to his neck, while the 12 who carry the twisted cord stand before

39. Olmec sculpture (Museum of Jalpa) with squatting figure eating ropes, identified here as the equivalent of the Egyptian god Aken.

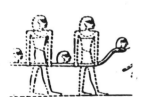

40b. The succeeding Egyptian god (here above) is called "the swallower".

40a. Egyptian papyrus painting of god Aken with figures symbolising the twelve hours of the night.

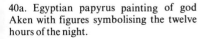

him (Ill. 40a). Strange as it may seem the Olmec representation is more true to the Egyptian text than the Egyptian picture which is iconographically incorrect in that the ropes should come out of the mouth and not be attached to the neck. As for the bizarre face of the Olmec Aken, it seems to have been borrowed from the text above the adjacent creature called "the swallower" (Ill. 40b), who is described as a serpent without eyes, nose or ears, a kind of non-articulated ophidian.

God 2 are the sky bearers. These Olmec atlantes excavated in Portrero Nuevo (Ill. 41) are by far the earliest in America. They survive in Maya myth as the four Bacab gods who escaped when the earth was destroyed by a deluge, and then upheld the four points of the world *(Tozzer, A.M.: 1941, pp. 135-6).* The Egyptian myth is identical: there were four supporters of the sky, and they were created in the primaeval waters *(Clark, R.T.R.: 1959, p. 85).* You may object that there are only two atlantes here. But if you look above you will see a symbol four times repeated. These are none other than the hieroglyph for "sky" in Egypt. Here for example is the sky goddess Nut supporting her sky sign (Ill. 42) *(Neugebauer, O. and Parker, R.A.: 1960, I, pl. 4).* So to conclude, in Egypt and in Mexico the mythology is the same, the artistic convention is the same, and the hieroglyph has the same meaning. In Egypt there was a festival to Amun called "Uplifting of the Sky" *(Wainwright, G.A.: 1934, pp. 145, figs. 3, 4).*

42. The Egyptian sky goddess Nut supporting the hieroglyphic sign for "sky".

41. Olmec Atlantis from Potrero Nuevo supporting a hieroglyph identified as the Egyptian sign for "sky" (repeated four times).

50

God 3. I identify the figure on an Olmec relief as the Egyptian god Bakhu (see Ill. 7). In Egyptian belief he is the mountain of the far western limits of the earth. *The Book of the Dead* says: "On the brow of that mountain is a serpent 30 cubits in length, 3 cubits of the front of which are of flint" *(Pritchard, J.B.: 1955, p. 12)*. My identification is not only based on the gigantic stone serpent on the brow of the personified mountain, but also because of the reed boat being upside down, just as in Egypt there are representations of the solar bark which are upside down (see p.15). One feature remains to be explained—it is the incense bag held in the hand of Bakhu. It was perhaps suggested by the Egyptian tale in which the shipwrecked sailor is given all sorts of incense by the prince of Punt, who is a gigantic serpent, once again measuring 30 cubits *(Erman, A.: 1966, pp. 29-35)*.

God 4 I identify as the Egyptian god Seth. In Egyptian mythology Seth attacks the demon who threatens the prow of the solar ship at sunset. This took place on the mountain of the far western boundaries of the earth. True Seth usually fights a serpent, but one text does describe his

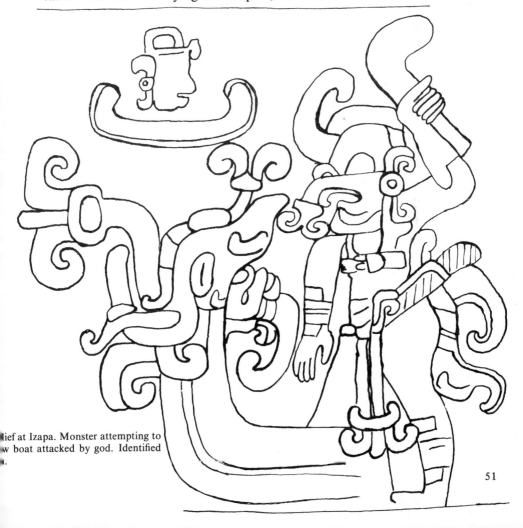

lief at Izapa. Monster attempting to
w boat attacked by god. Identified

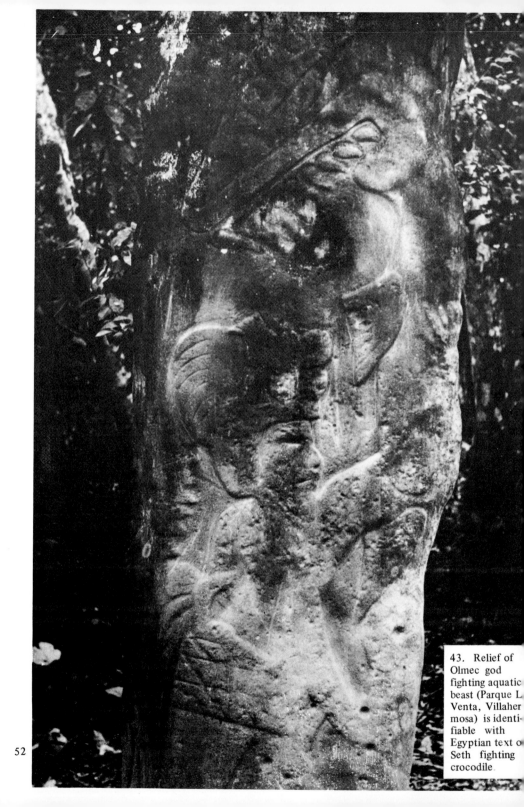

43. Relief of Olmec god fighting aquatic beast (Parque L Venta, Villaher mosa) is identifiable with Egyptian text o Seth fighting crocodile.

52

enemy as the crocodile god *(James, E.O.: 1958, p. 181),* and the monster baring its jaws on this Olmec relief at Villahermosa is a crocodile (Ill. 43). There is one anomaly—this is a hand-to-hand combat in the Babylonian manner. But in the light of the sequence of other Babylonian traits I have compiled indicating their presence in Mexico (see above p.22f) this feature can also be attributed to their intervention. Again one might object that while there is a god attacking a monster, there is no solar boat. But in this relief from Izapa (Ill. 44) toward the Pacific coast it is all there — the dragon, the slayer, and the little bark. The relief evokes the text of Rameses III who four times compares himself to "Seth slaying the robber-serpent on the prow of the evening bark" *(Edgerton, W.F. and Wilson, J.A.: 1936, pp. 38, 42, 57).*

God 5 is the baby Horus; you can call him "the solar child". He is described in the texts as "child of the sky who dawns in the bow of his ship, and sails with the king to the horizon in the bark of Ra" *(Allen, T. G.: 1916, pp. 29, 64, 28).* "He is Horus the child, the babe with the finger in his mouth" *(Mercer, S.A.B.: 1942, p. 130).* Here on this relief of Rameses III (Ill. 45) he is sitting on the prow of the sun's ship *(University of Chicago: 1953, pl. 421).* Supposing Rameses' solar ships reached the Far West of the World, what would be more likely than that the god on the prow should be much celebrated there. And hence I identify the child Horus with the Olmec figurines popularly called "baby face". The perforated star on the head of this one *(Metropolitan Museum of Art: 1970,*

45. Relief from Medinet Habu with solar god in boat, Seth fighting serpent, and the child Horus (sun-child) seated on prow.

46. Olmec baby-face terracotta figure with solar symbol on head.

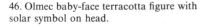

53

pl. 20) indicates his solar connection (Ill. 46). This figure still has his finger in his mouth, though in time the hand dropped when the meaning was forgotten. But Mexican literature never forgot that the sun was Tonatiuh, "the beautiful child" *(Caso, A.: 1967, 32-3)*. And here he is in Sahagun's vivid description: "Now thou causest the sun to appear, to come forth. Now once again thou art rejuvenated; thou emergest as a child. Once again thou becomest as a baby" *(Sahagun: 1969, Bk. 6, p. 32)*.

God 6 is Thoth (Ill. 47a), the patron god of scribes. On every expeditionary ship there would have been a scribe. And *The Book of the Dead* has Thoth as "the secretary of Ra in the solar bark" *(Boylan, P.: 1922, p. 58)*. Thoth has an ibis bill. This Olmec jade statuette from the Tuxtlas (Ill. 47b) has a duck's bill over his mouth, and on it is either a stylus for writing (it is poised just over the writing), or it is an ibis bill—it is notable that in Mexico the ibis was regarded as sacred *(Sahagun: 1950-63, Bk. 2, 32; ill. 89)*. Elsewhere I have shown the actual presence of an Egyptian scribe among the Olmecs (above p.40f), and there can be no doubt that he would have had his patron god with him. In fact Sahagun confirms that the ancestors who came in the dim past from across the sea and landed at Panotla (north of Vera Cruz) had among them wise men called Amoxoaque *(Sahagun: 1950-63, Bk. 10, 190)*, which has been translated "Book men" *(Carrasco, P.: 1971, p.460)*. You will notice that above the Long Count inscription, one of the two earliest in Mesomaerica, there is an introductory glyph which must mean 'sea' or 'ocean'.

47a. Egyptian god Thoth with ibis head, the god of writing.

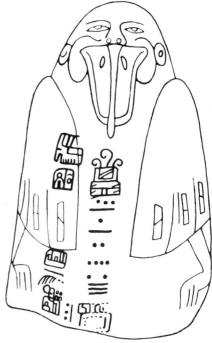

47b. One of the earliest known longcount inscriptions in Mexico with priest of god wearing a bird's mask (from the Tuxtlas, Mexican Gulf). Jade.

God 7 is "the Great Cackler". This duck basin from San Lorenzo is beautiful (Ill. 48), but looked at from the side it can mean nothing. But on the front is incised this duck with open mouth flying up as it were out of the waters of chaos (Ill. 49). *The Book of the Dead* describes just such a bird. It is "the Great Cackler, born of the Primaeval Waters in which the world was eclipsed" *(Clark, R.T.R.; 1959, p. 56)*. In other words it is the god who broke the silence, and brought speech into the world with a cackle. It is significant that in one instance this text is found right next to the sun's boat in an Egyptian temple *(Naville, E.: 1901, pt. 4, pl. CXV)*. I believe that this first event in creation was commemorated in one of the later Mexican festivals in which men jumped into the water and began to cackle like ducks and other birds *(Sahagun: 1950-63, Bk. 2, 77)*.

49. Front view of the same basin incised with duck flying up from the water. Identified here with "The Great Cackler".

50. Egyptian god Osiris lying prone with raised head signifying resurrection. (Cairo Museum).

51. Olmec sculpture lying prone with raised negroid head (originally from Tres Zapotes now at Santiago Tuxtla).

God 8 is Osiris. He appears in Mexico in two or three different forms. One of the forms of Osiris is that his body is extended along the earth, but he is reviving and raising his head, as in this Egyptian sculpture (Ill. 50) *(Daressy, G.: 1906, p. 114, no. 38, 424)*. The text says that this was when the boat of the sun passed his tomb in the seventh division of the Underworld *(Budge E.A.W.: 1906, III, p. 153)*. This negroid sculpture now in Santiago Tuxtla (Ill. 51) lies prone and raises his head exactly like the resurrected Osiris. Another form of Osiris is that he is upside down, and his body forms a loop (Ill. 52). The legend says "his circuit is the Tuat" or Underworld *(Budge, E.A.W.: 1904, I, p. 204)*. Notice how the feet of the god bend round and touch the head *(Budge, E.A.W.: 1899, p. 29)*, just as in early clay figurines from Central Mexico, especially from the Tlatilco cemetery (Ill. 53). If this were just an acrobat what would he be doing among the graves? I maintain that by emulating an attitude of Osiris, it was imagined that the deceased had become an incarnation of Osiris.

56

52. Egyptian papyrus painting with solar ship passing through the Underworld and Osiris in acrobatic pose.

53. Clay figurine from Tlatilco cemetery performing the same acrobatic feat as Osiris.

A third form of Osiris in Mexico is the Olmec sarcophagus having the representation of a jaguar with vegetation sprouting from its back *(Joralemon, P.D.: 1971, fig. 145, p. 50)*. In the Egyptian cult plants sprout out of the dead Osiris, the germination of seeds signifying revival of the dead *(Otto, E.: 1968, pp. 58, 24)*. But why the feline aspect? Because in Egypt too Osiris lies on a bed in the form of a lion *(Budge, E.A.W.: 1911, II, p. 26)*, and again the germinating bed in the Tomb of Neferhotpe identifies the deceased with Osiris, and calls him "the lion" *(Griffith, J.G.: 1966, pp. 109-10)*.

God 9 is The Silent One. This Olmec head in the Museum at Jalapa (Ill. 54) would seem to be another Underworld god, but he does not give much away. If what he has over his mouth is intended to be a pad, then his attribute must be that he is mute. And as such he can be linked up with Egyptian mythology. There is an Underworld god called "the Silent One", and texts speak of dead souls descending to his "domain of silence" *(Zandee, J.: 1960, pp. 93-4)*.

54. Enigmatic Olmec head possibly identifiable with "the Silent God" of the Egyptian Underworld. (Jalapa Museum).

55. Olmec god's head from Laguna de los Cerros (Jalapa Museum) with cranial hole (not visible here). Could symbolize the hole where the sun enters.

God 10 is the god of the crater. This is indicated by the hole in the cranium of this Olmec head from Laguna de los Cerros (Ill. 55). His hair is crinkly or negroid. I believe that the hole symbolized the "cavern" which the sun enters according to the Egyptian texts *(Piankoff, A.: 1964, p. 23)*, or "the falling place, the entering place of the sun", the *ciuatlampa*, according to Sahagun *(1969, Bk. 6, pp. 162-3)*.

I come now to the second category — the Egyptian gods who survive in diluted or distorted form in later Mexico, though there is every chance that their Olmec counterparts may be discovered some day.

God 11 is the Mexican fire god Huehueteotl. Sahagun describes him as the god "who is set in the navel of the earth, who lies in the turquoise enclosure" *(1950-69, Bk. 6, pp. 19, 88-9)*. This description comes from the Egyptian *Book of Day* in which the sun god Ra is described as rejoicing "in the mysterious region, and resting in the turquoise meadows" *(Piankoff, A.: 1954, p.391)*.

58

God 12 is the Egyptian sky goddess Nut. In *Codex Borgia* (Ill. 56) there occurs *(Marti. S.: 1971, p. 36)* what has been regarded as a personified cosmic tree. Her three main attributes are that she is an inverted female, her body splits in two, and she gives birth. Here on the ceiling of the Tomb of Rameses VI the inverted goddess Nut's body splits in two (Ill. 57), and again here the sun is born out of her vulva (Ill. 58), as the text expressly says *(Piankoff, A.: 1954, I, p. 390; II, pl. 113, 187)*. One attribute can be a coincidence—but a sequence of three?

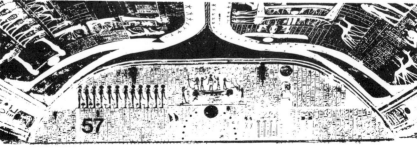

56. Tree goddess from *Codex Borgia* — an inverted female with split legs; giving birth.

57. Tomb painting of Rameses VI at Thebes with sky goddess on ceiling — her body splitting in two.

58. Painting from same tomb, with the goddess Nut giving birth to the sun.

God 13 is Quetzalcoatl. Though his origins are composite, at least three of his myths or traits have Egyptian parallels. Firstly his name—feathered serpent. This Egyptian underworld god (Ill. 59), twin serpent on one side and bearded on the other, is called "the many-coloured feathered one", or "he of dappled plumage" *(Piankoff, A.: 1954, p. 267)*. Secondly Quetzalcoatl was got drunk because he would *not* sacrifice humans, while in Egyptian myth Hathor was made drunk because she *was* destroying humans *(Piankoff, A.: 1955, pp. 28-9)*. Thirdly Quetzalcoatl went away across the seas on a serpent raft. The boat paddled by the dead in the Egyptian Underworld had serpents on both prow and stern *(Shorter, A. A.W.: 1937, p. 85)*.

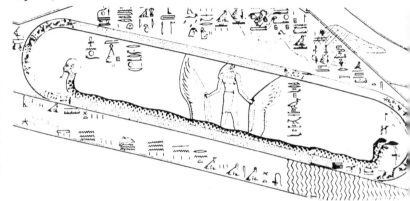

59. Egyptian papyrus painting of the Underworld god called "The Many Coloured Feathered One". He is equivalent to Quetzalcoatl, the Mexican god whose name means "the feathered serpent".

God 14 is the Egyptian Underworld god Sokar. He is the god standing on the back of the "many coloured feathered one" where he stretches out his hands to hold its wings. In Mexico he appears on a relief from Izapa *(Norman, V. Garth: 1973, pt. 1, pl. 21)*. The god with out-stretched arms is bearded and winged, and like Sokar stands on the back of a double-ended serpent (Ill. 60). His lower body is swallowed by a jaguar whose underworld attribute is indicated by the symbol of the contained cross.

61. Excavations within the Cholula pyramid have revealed a layer of painting below the painted plaster showing scenes of a grasshopper god drinking pulque, served by an attendant from a kind of amphora.

60. Stone sculpture from Izapa. Double-ended snake with stylized god's heads, has a winged figure standing on it with outstretched arms. The latter emerges from a beast marked with Underworld sign (a contained St. Andrew's cross).

God 15 is the grasshopper god. This god is found in the very early paintings discovered deep within the Cholula pyramid recently (Ill. 61), and not yet properly published. Why such importance attached to the grasshopper? Mexican mythology does not give any clear answer, but its Egyptian prototype tells us that in the heaven of Osiris lay a field of grasshoppers *(Budge, E.A.W.: 1904, II,pp. 120, 379).* Also that one of the Pharaohs flew up to heaven like the grasshopper of Ra *(Budge, E.A.W.: 1904, I, p. 445).* And finally the grasshopper is actually depicted as an occupant of the sun's boat *(Clark, R.T.R.: 1959, pp. 254-5).*

61

God 16 is the sun god Ra. The left half of this Tlatilco mask (Ill. 62a) has the protruding tongue of the later Mexican sun god. And the right half, since it is skeletal, must be the Underworld god. So here the sun and Underworld gods unite in one image. This idea stems from Egypt. In the Tomb of Rameses II the gods Osiris and Ra are fused in a single image (Ill. 62b) (only here one above the other instead of one beside the other), and the text says that each is completed in the other *(Clark, R.T.R.: 1959, pp. 158-9).* Also Rameses IV went out of his way to enquire about this, and was told that the two gods *did* unite in the Underworld *(Montet, P.: 1958, p. 298).* Though there is identity of conception there is no visual resemblance between the Egyptian prototype and its Mexican counterpart. I maintain that this was because the idea was transmitted orally.

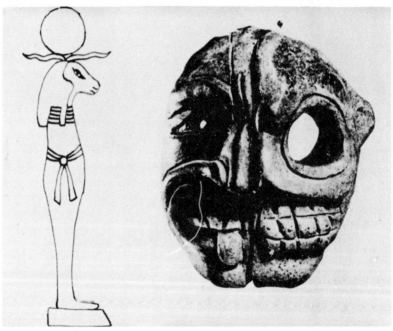

62b. Two Egyptian gods in one. Ra above and Osiris below, gods of Underworld and Sun.

62a. Terracotta mask from Tlatilco of Formative period combining sun and underworld gods in one image.

God 17 is the Mexican god of duality — Ometeotl. He was not represented because he was conceived of as being "invisible as night" *(Nicholson, I.: 1968, p. 114).* Now it so happens that the name of the Egyptian god Amon means just that—"the hidden" *(Wilson, J.A.: 1965, p. 130).* Does this not suggest that Ome is none other than Amon? Egyptian hymns intoned to Amon described his shrine as hidden, his name as hidden, and his image as hidden *(Pritchard, J.B.: 1955, pp. 336, 368).* Compare this with what the *Popol Vuh* tells us about the first people who came to this land from across the sea. They faced the sunrise, and sang the song called "it is hidden" *(Popol Vuh: 1971, 1, 6057f.)*.

God 18 is the Egyptian phallic god Min. I have already shown (above p. 47) that Min's deportment and gesture and his processional festival in which artificial phalluses were carried are both found in Mexico, and the phallic cult first appears in America in the Olmec period.

God 19 is the Mexican god of the Night Sky—Tezcatlipoca. According to myth he was knocked out of the sky with a cudgel, and he became the constellation of the Great Bear *(Caso, A.: 1967, pp. 29-30)*. He is depicted in the codices with a single sound leg, and a burning mirror attached to the other. I claim that Tezcatlipoca has his origins in the Egyptian constellation Mes, or the Great Bear (see Ill.92). In this Ramessid rendering of the stars the single-legged bull Mes is being attacked by the god An, and a trail of stars connects the leg of Mes to the mooring post on the earth *(Neugebauer, O. and Parker, R.A.: 1969, Text, 183, 185)*. To sum up: both gods are attacked in the sky, both have a single leg, both fall earthward, and both are identified with the same constellation.

God 20 is the Mexican goddess Tlazolteotl. She would eat the sins of men when they confessed to her once in their lifetime. Similarly this Egyptian monster Amemit was called "the devouress". She would eat the hearts of condemned sinners, after the dead had confessed to her at the Last Judgement *(Budge, E.A.W.: 1929, p. 23)*. Sahagun adds that accompanying her (Tlazolteotl) was a seer who had memorized knowledge and knew the sacred picture books *(Sahagun: 1950-63, Bk. I, p. 8-9)* —in fact an excellent description to the counterpart of the scribal god Thoth. We shall now see that all the three Egyptian gods connected with the Judgement of the Dead (Ill. 63) are present in Mexico—that is Amemit, Thoth and now

3. Judgement of the Dead being performed by Anubis weighing the souls of the dead. Thoth the scribal god recording, and Amemit the crocodile god waiting to devour the sinners.

63

God 21, the jackal god Anubis. Sahagun reports that the first people who came to this country brought with them from their land a god called Coyotlinauatl, whom they never ceased to worship *(Sahagun: 1880, pp. 587-9).* On festival days the image of this god was dressed in the skin of a coyote. In Egypt too the jackal mask was used in the Anubis ritual (Ill. 64) *(Morenz: 1965, p. 80, fig. 22).* And need I say that the prairie wolf is the nearest equivalent to a jackal. I would go further and modify the remark of Sahagun to the effect that the original inhabitants who came to this country not only brought with them this god, but all the twenty one I have mentioned.

64. Hollow terracotta mask from Egyp of the jackal god Anubis. It was meant t be worn by a priest for ceremonies a shown on left.

This will not seem astonishing if one remembers what the Maya text, the *Popol Vuh,* has to say. It says that the first people who came to their land came across the sea from the sunrise. It adds that they were seers, worshippers and sacrificers; they brought their scriptures with them, and the name of their god was changed after they had come. *(Popol Vuh: 1971, 1.5063-6, 5700f., 7221f.)*

Postscript
The Sun god, his phases and attributes

The Egyptian *Book of the Dead* claims that four gods constitute "the Western Souls". They are Sobek "the immortal", the Lord of Bakhu, Seth "the Lord of Life", and the Sun god Ra *(Pritchard, J.B.: 1955, p. 12).*

We have found the presence in Mexico of Seth and Bakhu (Gods 3 and 4), while the name Sobek the crocodile god could have survived as the crocodile Cipact in Mexico, which was one of the 20 days of the Aztec month, as has been observed *(Kelley, D.H.: 1962, p. 18)*. As for the sun god—we have seen him in his childhood state (God 5), in his fusion with the Underworld god (God 16), and in his hidden state (God 17). In the succeeding chapter we shall see the sun god in his setting manifestation (below p.69), and in his dead state (below p.74). And now we shall see four other aspects of the sun god which are encountered both in Egypt and in Mexico.

1.   Since in Egyptian mythology the sun continues its journey through the Underworld at night, this god was given a specific designation. This Night Sun, Af, is represented journeying in his bark at Medinet Habu (Ill.45). This unique conception of a night sun once again is found among the Mayas. He is the last of the nine lords of the Underworld, and he has on his head a cross sign on an oval disc *(Thompson, J.E.S.: 1960, cf. fig. 34, Nos. 46-57, and p. 210)*.

2.   An Egyptian text describes the eye of Ra kindling a fire that illuminates the dwellers in the Underworld *(Zandee, J.: 1969, p. 288)*. The fiery eye appears in Mexico in Olmec sculptures, and is admitted to be the attribute of one of the chief Olmec deities *(Joralemon, P.D.: 1971, p. 90)*. Olmec serpents have flame eyebrows, which may be compared with the Egyptian serpent Setmarf "he who has fire in his eye" *(Léfebure, E.: 1878, X, p. 115)*, or the uraeus serpents which are conceived as "the burning eye of Ra" *(Posener, G.: 1962, p. 291)*.

3.   The weeping eye is a characteristic of the Egyptian sun god. It is represented both in paintings *(Leclant, J.: 1954, Pl. XXIV)*, and in inscriptions where he is described as the "bodies of the Weeper" *(Piankoff, A.: 1964, p. 169)*, and as "the tears of the Glorious Eye" *Piankoff, A.: 1954, p. 169)*. This theme of the Weeping God was fairly widespread in Middle America. According to Las Casas a god with weeping eyes was adored in many parts of Guatemala *(Joyce, T.A.: 1913, p. 370)*. The weeping eye is characteristic of some gods in Mexico, but conspicuously not of the rain god Tlaloc *(Joyce, T.A.: 1913, cf. figs. 10-13, p. 372)*. In fact in Colombia it was characteristic of their sun god. At the harvest festival of the Chibchas men took part in masks painted with tears, and the chronicler states that these tears were meant as an appeal to the pity of the sun *(Joyce, T.A.: 1913, pp. 366-68)*.

4.   On the West wall of a hall at Medinat Habu is a hymn to the setting sun *(University of Chicago: 1953, pls. 421-2)*, with the bark of Atum being towed through the open door of the sky. The Aztecs not only have a conception of the sun at the horizon, Tlachitonatiuh who rules one of the days of the week of their 260 day calendar *(Thompson, J.E.S.: 1943, p. 119)*, but they also have the conception of the

setting of the afternoon sun, Cuauhtemoc symbolised by the eagle *(Caso, A.: 1947, p. 11)*. The introductory picture of the Mexican book *Codex Laud (Burland, C.: 1966, p. 22)* has an eagle arriving at the crater where the sun goes down (Ill. 65). The picture recalls the Egyptian text in which Horus described himself as the great falcon whose "flight has reached the horizon . . . to the ramparts of the house of the hidden name" *(Clark, R.T.R.: 1959, p. 216)*. The Mexican picture has a god seated in a ring with solar rays, and into this obtrudes the way to the Underworld. There at the edge, the Underworld god Mictlantecuhtli is sacrificing a human. This same sequence is described in the *Book of Caverns* in the Tomb of Rameses VI: Ra opens the gate of the sky and enters into darkness; then the enemies of Osiris (the Underworld god) are beheaded in the place of annihilation *(Piankoff, A.: 1954, Texts, p. 53)*.

65. Mexican Codex with solar eagle arriving at entrance to the Underworld, the *ciuatlampa*. On the right the Underworld god performing human sacrifice (victim omitted here).

To conclude, we have found nine different manifestations of the sun god which are common to the mythologies of Egypt and Middle America, which are scarcely if at all found anywhere else. These are descriptions of the sun god as a child, as fused with the god of the Underworld, as hidden, as opening up the double doors of the West, as dead, as the night sun, as the fiery eye, as the weeping eye, and as the eagle reaching the West.

Further identical solar conceptions include the union with the sun disc (see p. 11), the journey with the sun across the sky (see p. 11), and the goddess who holds the sun in her arms, and takes it down into the West (see p. 80).

PART 7

Egypt's Underworld in Mexico

In the Far West of the World where the sun goes down lay the entrance to Egypt's Underworld. If this is remembered—all doors open literally and figuratively. The evidence for Egypt in Mexico is so precise and so prolific that it is quite amazing why no one has stumbled on it up to now. Perhaps one of the reasons is that there is a stylistic difference. But this is because those who went across were priests, slaves and naval mercenaries, and could teach what they knew orally, but not execute the works themselves. Then there are slight anomalies and aberrations. Surely one should expect this in view of the factors of time and space. And then again because of the accidents of discovery the evidence is scattered and has to be ferreted. But I do not wish to make excuses. On the contrary I believe that if you look at the conceptions and not at their outward semblance, those transmitted are sometimes more faithful than even their prototypes which suffer from the strictures of convention. I predict that the time is at hand when in order to understand New Kingdom Egypt fully, we will have to turn as well to the evidence in Mexico.

Why is it that I have been able to see the Egyptian presence on the Vera Cruz coast writ large, and no one has seen it before? Because I have found the key—what it is these Egyptians were looking for. And it is corroborated by Sahagun who says that the first settlers who came to Mexico came across the sea, and they came looking for a terrestrial paradise—"Esta gente venia en demanda del paraiso terrenal" (see p. 8).

In the Egyptian Underworld is a paradise called Iaru or Yaru, and we have seen the relief on which Rameses III is paddling his boat in its waters (Ill. 7). He is also reaping the barley which grows with exceptional vigour there. Since this barley is such a conspicuous feature of this land, and its dimensions are given in meticulous detail, it is probable that the Mexican conception of the Underworld being "a house of corn"—Cincalco—is directly derivative. But this identification has to be viewed against all that follows.

Notice how Rameses is seated in his boat with one leg tucked under him, and the other folded above. This is precisely the manner in which the Olmec figure from St. Martin now in Jalapa Museum (Ill. 66) is seated. He is holding a bar in his hands which could be a truncated oar. There is a cross on the end of it, as also over his head, reminiscent of the cross symbols over Rameses's head which evidently refer to the celestial city. The oar was truncated either because it was no longer needed—in the Egyptian conception boats in the Underworld were not rowed but towed, or it was a manner of indicating that they had decided not to return (for which one can suggest a number of perfectly good reasons).

66. Stone sculpture found in crater of St. Martin Pajapan near Mexican Gulf. Figure wearing raised jaguar mask holds a bar, conceivably stump of oar truncated and marked with a cross on the end. A similar sculpture has now been found at La Venta. Both places interpreted here as simulated ritual entrances to the Underworld.

67b. Sarcophagus of Seti I with the sun boat (darkened here) heading for the two peaks of the Western mountain. (Now Sir John Soane Museum, London).

This Olmec sculpture was found inside the crater of a dormant volcano which must have been adopted as a ritual entrance to the Underworld. In Mexican conception this would be the *ciuatlampa,* "the falling place, the entering place of the sun" *(Sahagun: 1969, Bk. 6, p. 162-3).* In Egyptian conception it would be the cavern which the sun enters *(Piankoff, A.: 1964, p. 23).* The crater of St. Martin Pajapan lies about five miles from the Mexican Gulf, and rises to a height of 1200 metres above sea level, which makes it the most conspicuous eminence of the Tuxtla range. There are two peaks, one north and the other south. Now compare this (Ill. 67a) *(Medellin Zenil: 1968, p. 9f.)* with the two peaks at the Far West of the World toward which the sun's boat sails in Egyptian representations, as in the relief from the sarcophagus of Seti I (Ill. 67b) *(Bonomi & Sharpe: 1864, pls. 4-5).* This scene is a prelude to the description of the different parts of the Underworld.

67a. Profile of the crater of San Martin Pajapan with its two peaks. It lies about 4-5 miles from the Mexican Gulf.

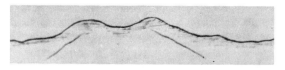

Its Mexican counterpart is to be found in *Codex Vaticanus* (Ill. 4). Here again there is a prelude. The first stage is "on the earth", the second a "water passage" which has the head of an animal crossing the sea, and the third is the actual entrance called "Where the hills clash together". A figure is as if pushing open the two hills. This is almost a literal rendition of the New Kingdom Sun Hymns which speak of the sun god "who openst up the double doors of the nether world" *(Stewart, H.M.: 1967, p. 69).* In another Egyptian text the *"Book of Caverns",* Ra says "I open the gate of the sky in the West . . . behold I have entered into the West, I have passed through the first Cavern" *(Piankoff, A.: 1954, pp. 49-50).*

We will pass by the other stages (because they seem to me to be local and historical happenings)—the fourth "where a hill is being quarried for obsidian knives", the sixth where "the banners are unfurled", the seventh where "someone is riddled with arrows", and the ninth "the place of the dead where the streets are on the left". This leaves the fifth stage which is "the place of the obsidian-bladed wind", to which we shall return in a moment, and the eighth "where someone's heart is eaten". Here from the second division of the same Egyptian "Book of Caverns" we have a scene of the enemies of the sun god with their hearts at their feet (Ill. 68). The text calls them "the bloody ones with torn-out hearts in the Place of Destruction" *(Piankoff, A.: 1954, p. 64).* The extraordinary Mexican practice of plucking out the heart in connection with the sun cult could have its origins here.

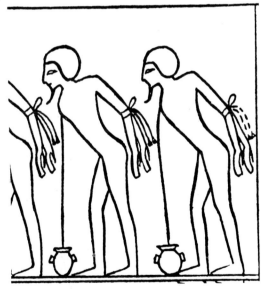

68. Egyptian representation of the enemies of the sun god with their hearts plucked out in the Underworld. Compare the Mexican Underworld Stage 8 (III.4) with the heart being devoured, and the Mexican human sacrifice in which the heart was plucked out and offered to the sun.

There are few points in common between the stages of the Mexican Underworld as presented by Sahagun *(Sahagun: 1950-69, Bk. 3, p. 41 and Appendix)*, and that illustrated in the *Codex Vaticanus*. But both have a stage called "place of the obsidian-bladed wind". In Egyptian conception one of the stages is called "city gate with sharp knives" *(Piankoff, A.: 1955, p. 85)*. What is the obsidian blade, but a sharp knife?

For the remainder of the stages we will stay with Sahagun, and compare them with their counterparts in the two Egyptian texts *The Book of Gates* and *The Book of what is in the Netherworld (Budge, E.A.W.: 1906, I, p. 160; III, pp. 109, 116, 127, 131)*. The second division in both Egypt and Mexico is guarded by a large serpent. In view of the exact correspondence of the first two stages this can scarcely be a coincidence.

The third stage in Sahagun was guarded by an alligator, while the seventh in Egypt was a crocodile. Sahagun's Xochitonal has also been translated "green lizard" *(Nicholson, H.B.: 1971, Table 2)*. This Olmec sculpture of a crocodile now at Villahermosa (Ill. 69) is of greenish stone, and hence may be Xochitonal. There is over its backbone an incised stylized face. So also in Egyptian conception the head of Osiris arises out of the back of the lizard god (Ill. 70) *(Budge, E.A.W.: 1906, I, p. 25; cf. p. 159)*. Or again the text says the Eye comes out of the backbone of the crocodile "Evil of Lake" the moment he hears the voice of the barge of Ra *(Piankoff, A.: 1954, pp. 283-4; fig. 80)*.

69. Olmec sculpture of crocodile in greenish stone at Villahermosa. Incised over its backbone is a head not visible here; also a hole.

70. "Lizard god" in the Egyptian Underworld with the head of Osiris on its backbone.

The fourth stage in Sahagun was "eight deserts" or plains. The fourth in Egypt was a desert region called Seker, and it was supported by two human-headed sphinxes called Af *(Budge, E.A.W.: 1906, III, p. 135)*. This Olmec sculpture again at Villahermosa (Ill. 71) undoubtedly represents a sphinx. This is surprising enough to find in Mexico, but as it is serving as a support I identify it with the desert Seker.

In the fifth stage in Egypt was 'the god swallowing the hours', and I have already identified him in an Olmec sculpture earlier (see p. 49).

The sixth stage was as we have just seen the obsidian blades whose equivalent is sharp knives.

The seventh is Osiris lifting his head, whose presence I have already shown (see p. 56).

The eighth is the watery paradise of Tlalocan as depicted in the Tepantitla Palace in Teotihuacan (Ill. 72). The figures swim and dive in the watery mountain. Compare the Egyptian text which describes the region of the Underworld in which the submerged ones swim for survival, enjoy the coolness of the waters, and move toward the primaeval flood *(Piankoff, A.: 1954, I, p. 194)*. At Teotihuacan one of the figures wears a life belt over his shoulder. Another who is wearing one is rescuing a man who is drowning. Such U-shaped reed lifebelts were worn by Egyptian sailors (Ill. 73), and as far as I know are found nowhere else. I claim that the

74. Stone yoke carved with representation of what appears to be a frog. Museo Nacional, Mexico City.

enigmatic *yugos* of Mexican art are remembrances of these not only because of their shape, but because they are usually green (denoting the sea), and because one of the yokes found *in situ* in the Vera Cruz region was resting over the shoulders of the deceased *(Bernal, I. and Seuffert: 1970, pp. 7, 11)*. Some yokes have frogs represented on the front (Ill. 74), and this once again leads to Egypt where frogs were associated with the reed mats hanging from the prow of the sun's ship, and in this context the frogs were symbols of "one who repeats life" *(Thomas, E.: 1959, p. 45f.)*.

To return to the eighth stage of the Underworld the Egyptian texts describe its inhabitants as bathing, floating, swimming and diving *(Léfebure, E.: 1878, p. 124)*, and stylized figures are literally represented in this manner (Ill. 75) *(Piankoff, A.: 1954, I, fig. 54)*. There is no compositional scene, and no attempt to portray the "primaeval flood". On the other hand the derivative Mexican version has a vivid rendering of it, and hence is implicitly faithful to the Egyptian text.

75. Egyptian Underworld scene where the deceased float and swim without drowning.

72. Wall painting from the Tepantitla Palace in Teotihuacan representing the watery paradise Tlalocan. Note figure on right with U-shaped lifebelt. (above)

73. Egyptian sailor on papyrus boat with lifebelt over shoulder.

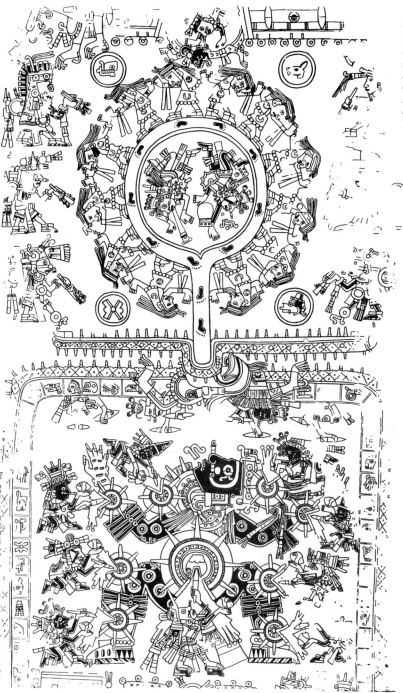

76. Mexican book *Codex Borgia*. Below, the sun god is sacrificed and is dead. Above, the 12 Ciuateteos perform a dance around his circuit denoted by his footprints.

Sahagun and *Codex Vaticanus* both stop short at stage nine which is described as "place of the dead". But the Egyptian scheme of the Underworld has twelve stages, and I shall now show that these last stages are represented in *Codex Borgia (Seler, E.: 1904-06: pls. 34, 39)*, and shall enumerate their contact with Egypt:

1. In the Codex is the darkened sun Youaltecutli (Ill. 76). He is dead, because his breath and speech are cut off. Toward the last stages in the Egyptian *Book of that which is in the Underworld* Re is conceived as the dead old sun god *(Budge, E.: 1904, I, pp. 257-8)*.

2. In the Codex the dead sun is being revived by fire on a hearth from which a child is springing (Ill. 77). An Egyptian text refers to the refilling of the solar disc with fire during the night *(Piankoff, A.: 1955, p. 94)*.

3. In the Codex the footprints of the sun god show that he has been through the body of the Fire Serpent. In the Egyptian Book cited above the boat of the sun is hauled through the body of the serpent *(Budge, E.A.W.: 1904, I, p. 258; 1906, I, 259)*.

4. In the Codex 12 Ciuateteos or sceptre women assist in the birth and revival of the sun. In Egyptian myth 12 women called Amkhiu tow the rope of the sun's boat and assist it on the paths of the sky *(Budge, E.A.W.: 1904, loc cit.)*.

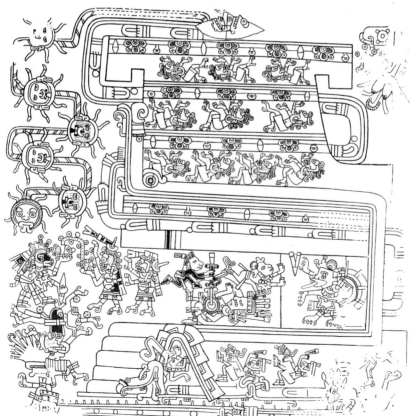

77. *Codex Borgia*. The earth dragon forms a shrine. From its hearth a child springs forth and becomes the sun. The Ciuahpipiltin draw the sun through the coils. At the top the sun appears as a stone knife and despatches the Tzitzimime.

5. In the Codex the tail of the serpent terminates on top in a red god whose head emerges from a stone knife. As though cut by the knife and tumbling down in loops is the multi-headed demon of darkness Tzitzimime—"those who fell headfirst". In Egyptian myth Apothis (also called Sessi) attempts to prevent the sun from rising, and Ra despatches it so that Apophis "plunges into the depths of the Abyss with face overturned" *(Clark, R.T.R.: 1959, pp. 209-10).*

6. In Egypt a text of Rameses III describes the helpers of the sun dancing and singing for him, and praising and shouting *(Daressy, G.: 1897, pp. 159-60).* And from *The Book of the Dead* it appears that homage and acclamations were actually made at dawn *(Budge, E.A.W.: 1898, III, p. 10).* Similarly in Mexico Sahagun tells us that dead warriors brought forth, gladdened, and cried out to the emerging sun *(Sahagun: 1969, Bk. 6, pp. 162, 164).* That this like all the rest came from Egypt is indirectly confirmed by the Maya text the *Popol Vuh* which speaks of a dance at sunrise performed by the ancestors who came across the sea from the East *(Popol Vuh: 1971, 5937-9, 6039).*

Section 2

If the migrants brought over their conceptions of the Underworld, they would have brought their funerary customs as well. There is again considerable evidence of this. For example we are told that in Mexico the priests delivered bunches of papers to the dead telling them that this would enable them to survive the encounters in the Underworld *(Sahagun: 1950-69, Bk. 3, p. 41).* In Egypt too the dead were buried with small sheets or strips of papyrus. On these were inscribed such texts as the *Book of Traversing through Eternity (Budge, E.A.W.: 1929, p. 13).*

Then again we know that in ancient Egypt mourning was for at least 70 days, and if during that time they went out of their house they smeared their faces with mud—just as the groaning women mourners put mud on theirs *(Montet, P.: 1958, pp. 316, 318).* When the Aztecs mourned their dead the chanters came dressed in dirty clothes and chanted the "song of dirt". The women did not wash their clothes, faces, or head until 80 days had gone by *(Duran: 1964, pp. 172-3).*

The stone sarcophagus with lid appears for the first time in the Americas in the Olmec context *(see Bernal, I.: 1968, pls. 27a, 44).* In Egypt the goddess Nut was as it were the patron goddess of the sarcophagus, and is frequently represented in or on it. In the *Pyramid Texts* she is actually called Coffin, Sarcophagus and Sepulchre *(Piankoff, A.: 1955, p. 21).* Similarly the Aztec goddess Micapetlacalli was called "the box of death" *(Caso, A.: 1967, p. 64).* The sarcophagus with lid survives in the Maya pyramid at Palenque.

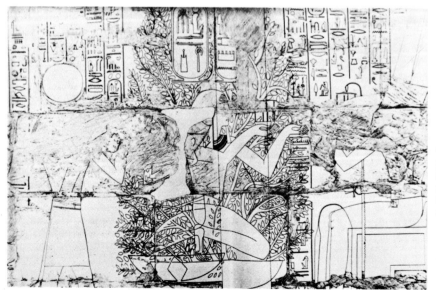

78. Sarcophagus in the Pyramid at Palenque (replica in National Museum). Relief on lid interpreted as deceased lying under the Yaxche tree.

The lid of the Palenque sarcophagus has the representation of a figure lying at the base of a schematized tree (Ill. 78). The tree is sometimes said to be the "world-directional tree". I maintain that it is the Yaxche. For Landa tells us that in Maya belief the dead rest forever under the great cool shade of the Yaxche, which is the ceiba *(Tozzer, A.M.: 1941, p. 131)*. Compare this with the Egyptian belief that the deceased lies under the shade of the sycamore tree *(Zabkar, L.V.: 1968, p. 140)*. There is also another underworld tree in Egyptian mythology, the tree of life called the Ished tree, and Rameses III for example is seated under it, while two gods write his name on its leaves (Ill. 79) *(University of Chicago: 1963, VI, pt. 2,*

79. Relief at Medine Habu of Rameses II in the midst of the tree on whose leave the gods write hi name.

pl. 448). This conception of the dead lying under the shade of a tree in the next world is, as far as I know, exclusive to Egypt and Mexico. My conclusion therefore is that the Mexican conceptions of Cincalco, Tlalocan and the Yaxche are all of Egyptian origin. And it could be that the name Yaxche is none other than Ished (cf. *Ya-xch-e* with *I-sh-ed).*

The typical attitude of the dead ruler in Egypt is with arms crossed over his chest. This attitude appears in Mexico, and this sculpture at the Museum of Jalapa (Ill. 80) is probably by far the earliest such. He is wearing a typical Egyptian wig. But while it is not certain that this is the

80. Sculpture at Jalapa Museum. Figure crosses arms on chest, fingers open in a curious way (as if his sceptres had been snatched away?).

81. Sculpture from Oaxaca of a man with curling moustachios — deceased with arms crossed in the Egyptian fashion. Now in Museo Nacional.

82. Mummy of Rameses III with arms crossed over chest fingers open.

representation of a deceased person, another such Olmecoid statue from Juchitan in Oaxaca must be so, since his rib cage indicates that he is dead (Ill. 81). The manner in which his hands are open and reach up to his shoulders, is a special characteristic of the Ramessid period *(Elliot Smith, G. and Dawson, W.R.: 1924, fig. 27, pp. 104-5)*. Compare this with the mummy of Rameses III (Ill. 82).

The identity of the sculptures of Olmec dignitaries seated in niches (Ill. 83) can once again be solved by referring to Egyptian texts. They are the horizon dwellers, the deceased who have made their seat among the westerners *(Zabkar, L.V.: 1968, p. 131)*. They are "lords of the caverns in their holes", and they are stated to hold ropes in their hands *(Zabkar, L.V.: 1968, p. 125)*. The Olmec figure holds a rope in his hands, but for a different reason. He has a flame headdress, and this is explained by the Egyptian spell which speaks of "the flame which comes from the horizon-dwellers" *(Borghouts, J.E.: 1971, I, p. 348)*.

83. Olmec dignitary seated below mouth of a jaguar marked by a cross. He has a flame headdress and holds a rope. Villahermosa.

I maintain that among the funerary rites, the Egyptians introduced the ceremony of "the opening of the mouth" into Mexico. The ceremony being enacted in the wall painting in the Cave at Juxtlahuaca is such a scene, and I have shown the parallels (above p.26). The *Popol Vuh* tells us that the people who came across the sea from the sunrise would anoint the mouth of one of the idols with the blood of deers and birds, and at once the stone would speak *(Popol Vuh: 1971, 6249-55)*. This again is directly comparable to the Egyptian practice in which the bleeding foreleg of a bull could be touched to the mouth of a mummy or a statue to give it back its speech *(Budge, E.A.W.: 1901, pp. 192, 195)*. The Olmec were-jaguar has his mouth pressed open, and once again this appears to be a literal interpretation of the Egyptian ceremony. One indication of this is the two drill holes, one in each corner of the mouth, recalling the Egyptian text which speaks of the mouth of Osiris being pressed apart with the priest's two little fingers: "Thy mouth has been drawn apart for thee". *(Budge, E.A.W.: 1909, I, pp. 40, 80, 88)*.

I also believe that a form of the Egyptian conception of the *ka* survives in Mexican belief. The Egyptians believed that ancestors dwelt in the West, and their *kas* came forward to welcome the new arrival *(Schweitzer, U.: 1957)*. In the same way the Aztecs celebrated a feast to the dead once a year, and called on their ancestors to "come soon for we await you" *(Brinton, D.G.: 1896, p. 298)*. I claim that the figure of what looks like a petrified man at the Museum of Villahermosa with its arms stretched out in front (Ill. 84) is the *ka* of a mountain, and is an interpretation of the Egyptian text: "The mountain will hold out its arms, and the living *kas* will accompany him" *(Clark, R.T.R.: 1959, p. 233)*.

As for the Egyptian conception of a goddess of the horizon holding out her arms to take the sun down in the mountains (Ill. 85), as represented in pictures *(Piankoff, A.: 1957, fig. 25; Smith, W.S.: 1958, pl. 166a)*. this idea is preserved intact in Sahagun *(1950-69: Bk. 6, p. 163)*. He speaks of women who lived at the falling place of the sun who carried the sun in their hands, and brought it down, and left it where it enters the Underworld.

84. Terracotta with incisions giving effect of petrified wood. Interpreted as the *Ka* of a mountain which receives dead souls.

85. Egyptian representation of the Goddess of the West receiving the sun and taking it down into the Western mountain.

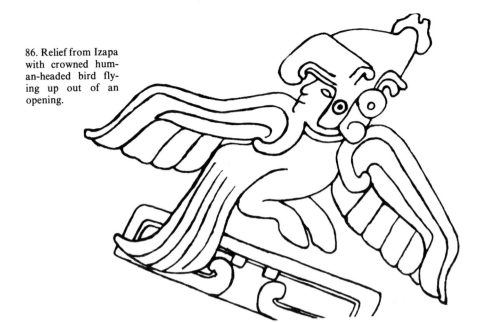

86. Relief from Izapa with crowned human-headed bird flying up out of an opening.

While the *ka* appears in Eastern Mexico, the Egyptian *ba* occurs on the West Coast. On a relief at Izapa a human-headed bird flies up out of an opening (Ill. 86) *(Norman, V. Garth: 1973, pl. 58)*, just as in an Egyptian tomb painting a *ba* bird representing the soul of a deceased flies up out of a hole in the tomb (Ill. 87) *(Posener, G.: 1962, p. 267)*. Few would doubt that the same conception is implied in both.

87. Egyptian papyrus painting with Ba bird flying up out of a hole in the tomb. The Ba is the soul of the deceased, and has freedom to come and go.

And there is still another Egyptian conception which was transmitted. It is that in the Underworld the deceased becomes "a glorious one" *(Piankoff, A.: 1934, p. 59)*. According to the *Popol Vuh* (7154) when the ancestor who had come across the sea from the sunrise died, he left behind his sign, his essence called "the shrouded glory", though this was given a visible form.

And finally there is a case for mummification. Take the squatting mummy bundles like this one from Coixtlahuaca in Western Mexico. It is wrapped in mats, and has a portrait mask over the face (Ill. 88). (Such portrait masks first appear in Olmec times). Compare the manner of burial of a Libyan tribe of the 19th Dynasty in Saqqara. A realistic mask covers the head and shoulders, and the body is wrapped in a mat of palm reeds tied with cords *(Goneim, Z.: 1956, pp. 54-5)*. Sahagun describes the Mexican dead as being "bound well, wrapped round and round, and tied firmly" *(Sahagun: 1950-63, Bk. 3, p. 41)*, a description that would fit the Egyptian practice better than any other. And finally Bancroft claims that evisceration was known in Mexico, and that bowels were taken out and replaced by aromatic substances *(Bancroft, H.H.: 1883, II, pp. 603-4)*.

The evidence presented in this Chapter for Mexican contact with Egypt is massive. Can a myriad precisely coinciding details be explained away by a convergence? And what are these details — not discrete and isolated, but a complex making a grand pattern. And what is this pattern? That the Egyptians sought and achieved their paradise, and this paradise was Mexico.

88. Mummy bundle from Tomb at Coixtlahuaca, Western Mexico it is wrapped in mats and rope and wears a portrait mask. Museo Nacional.

PART 8
Continued Search For Paradise

I shall now attempt to reconstruct from archaeological and literary evidence the events that followed when the Egypto-Olmecs discovered that Mexico could not be the Underworld they had been sent to find. Certainly some of the priests and expeditionary crew were prepared to be reconciled, and to make-believe that this was indeed "the sacred land". The many traces of Egyptian Underworld belief in Mexico which I have collected in the previous chapter are proof of this. As I see it, the evidence for a literal and tangible Underworld among the Olmecs include the crater of San Martin which was imagined as its entrance, the mound of La Venta which was a surrogate entrance for the sun, and the cave of Juxtlahuaca which was a simulated Underworld shrine where mysterious rites took place.

The disillusionment of the migrants is vividly portrayed in the Epic of the Quiche Maya, *the Popol Vuh*. It describes how their ancestors set out in search of the sun, came across the sea from the East, did not find what they were looking for, and decided to go away and continue their search leaving others behind (see above p. 39). They were looking for the dawning of the sun *(Popol Vuh: 1971, 6057f.)*. It seems to me that this vigil for the sunrise is reflected in the oldest monuments of Guatemala where, for example at Monte Alto, the pyramid and platform are thought to be aligned as though for observing the sunrise*(Shook: 1971, p. 72)*. Sahagan confirms *(1950-63, Bk.10, p. 190)* that the ancestors who had landed at Panotla did not remain long, but went to Guatemala. They too were searching, for they went looking at mountains (to find the mountain in which the sun would set?). It seems to me that this pattern of the Egypto-Olmecs landing and settling on the Gulf, and others going on across the country and to the south, is just what did occur. There are admitted to be archaeological traces of "a path of civilisation from the Gulf Coast to Guatemala", though at present this cannot be accurately plotted *(Baudez: 1971, p. 84)*.

Another passage in the *Popol Vuh (1971, 4695f.)* relates "Having completely conquered all of Hell (that is in my scheme the Egypto-Olmecs conquering most of Mexico as evidenced by widespread Olmec colonisation and trade network), they then walked into the sky, and one is the sun and the other of them is the moon. . . There climbed also the 400 sons who had been killed by Alligator . . . so now they became their companions : they became the stars of the sky".

This conception of the dead becoming stars stems from the Egyptian *Pyramid Texts* which calls the glorious dead "the Imperishable Ones", and "the eternal stars" *(Highbarger, E.L. 1940, p. 10)*. Moreover the journey of the solar barque is stated in hymns of the New Kingdom to be accomplished by the stars *(Stewart, H.M. 1967, p. 38)*. Since the Ramessid expedition to Mexico was undertaken as a solar voyage as I have shown, the expeditionary members were entitled to become stars of the sky. Viewed in this way the passage in the *Popol Vuh* of the conquerors being raised to the status of stars makes perfect sense, and no alternative explanation can compete with it. We shall see at the end of this chapter how this Egyptian conception of apotheosis to the sky was translated into 'reality' in America.

There are indications that the search did not end in Guatemala, but continued on. It is quite probable that their next presence is attested in San Salvador. Father Alonso Ponce heard of the myth that 400 youths rushed into a lake in the vicinity of San Miguel volcano and perished *(Seler, E. 1901-02, p. 112)*. Here is surely a reminiscence of the 400 sons walking into the sky? Why should they rush into a lake unless they were still seeking a mythical lake in the Underworld? Once again we shall see that they did discover such a lake in the last stage of their wanderings.

The reason for believing that their throwing themselves in the lake was only a symbolical gesture is that the trail leads beyond San Salvador into Costa Rica. Here the cult of apotheosis into stars recurs, though once again its significance has not been properly understood. Sometimes in dense jungle, sometimes on hill tops, often miles from their quarries are found the ancient stone balls. Many are almost perfectly spherical, and some are as much as 8 feet in diameter and are 8 tons in weight. A few native archaeologists suspect that they were connected with a star cult, and the natives themselves call them "skyballs" *(Von Daniken, E.: 1968, p. 85)*, and I maintain that this is quite correct. But the fact that some stone balls served as cemetery boundaries *(Stone, Doris: 1958, p. 45)*, is an even clearer indication that it was their way of saying that the deceased had become stars. As for the fashion of representing stars as spheroids, this was the usual manner of representing them in Egyptian star maps (see Ill. 92). Finally it should be noted that large stone balls were excavated in Mexico at the Olmec site of San Lorenzo (one a sphere 115 inches in circumference), and the excavator was reminded of those of Costa Rica *(Stirling, M.: 1955, p. 15)*.

We have so far traced the Egyptian migrants in their trek from Mexico to Guatemala to San Salvador to Costa Rica. And now we shall see their presence in Ecuador and Peru. In June 1965 man-made underground galleries were found in the Province of Morona-Santiago in Ecuador *(Von Daniken, E.: 1973)*. Though not as yet properly published it is evident that the working of the masonry is exceptionally fine, and could not have been executed by savages or even possibly by any known native peoples then residing in Ecuador. That the underground galleries were intended for living is suggested by the double ventilator shafts that appear at intervals. It is therefore reasonable to conceive the galleries as a kind of imagined Underworld.

It seems that at each stopping place some of the migrants stayed behind while others went on in their search for Paradise. In Peru and Northern Bolivia finally they felt that they had reached their goal, for there is no further trace of them beyond. I maintain that they were an element of the Chavin dynasty in Peru, since both Olmec and Egyptian ideas are found in abundance in this context. Since many of the ideas are *visibly* transmuted, and the correspondence is more marked *conceptually,* it would seem that the migration had taken well over a generation or two.

At Chavin de Huantar high in the Andean mountains they continued their attempt to build an Underworld shrine. Again there is a network of covered galleries on different levels consisting of cells, ramps and storerooms, and again the ventilation was through overhead ducts *(Guillermo Lumbreras: 1971, pp. 3-4).* And in the center of the complex was an obelisk, or at least that is what it is generally called. Obelisks are also claimed to have stood outside of the temple of Tiahuanaco and in front of the Pyramid of the Moon at Puma Puncu *(Honoré, P.: 1963, pp. 160-1, fig. 17).* The obelisk at Chavin de Huantar is in the form of an anthropomorphic knife. In Egypt the sun god Ra was called a "knife" (because he killed his nocturnal enemy each dawn), and again in Mexico the sun god was portrayed in this identical role, and is actually depicted as a stone knife (see above p.75). The Egyptian obelisk was a symbol of the sun god Ra, and the Peruvian obelisks would appear to be by analogy symbols of the sun in the Underworld.

An indication that the Egyptian obelisk had been introduced in Peru is that in one example as late as Inca times it was connected with a solar temple and covered with gold. We know from Juan de Batanzos that in the centre of the great square or court of the Temple of the Sun at Cuzco was a stone pillar shaped like a sugar loaf, pointed at the top and covered with gold leaf *(Westropp, H.M. and Wake, C.S.: 1970, p. 84).* So also in Egypt in the 18th-19th and following Dynasties the tops of the obelisks dedicated to the sun were coated with gold or electrum, and the smaller obelisks may also have had their shafts covered with gold plates *(Budge, E.A.W. 1926, pp. 37-8).*

In connection with the stone knives, the question arises - who were victims of the sun god? I believe they are the barbarous natives whose stone heads are tenoned into the external wall of the temple at Chavin. I would point out that the antecedents of this practice are the stone heads of enemies projecting from the walls of the buildings of Rameses III in Egypt.

It is in the Chavin context that gods are first represented in ancient Peru. Hence the close kinship with ancient Egypt cannot be a coincidence. Indeed the so-called staff god of Chavin and Tiahuanaco (Ill. 89) is closely paralleled in Egypt by the figure holding a pair of staffs surmounted by miniature gods. In one instance c.1250 B.C. the gods are identifiable as Ptah and Ammon-Ra (Ill. 90) *(Scamuzzi, E.: 1965, pl.LXXIV).* Rameses III holds a staff surmounted by a ram *(Legrain, E.: 1909, II, pls.XII,XIII),*

89. Relief of staff god from "Gate of the Sun" at Tihuanaco, Bolivia. It has head with solar rays, eyes with tear ducts, and stands on a stepped pedestal.

90. Staffs surmounted by the god of Creation and the Sungod from New Kingdom Egypt. Possible prototype of the Peruvian staff god.

which evidently symbolizes the creative power of the sun god *(Piankoff, A.: 1955, p. 95)*. Very recently the Olmec site of Xochipala in Mexico has yielded what has been described as a staff with a human face *(Gay, Carlo T.E.: 1971, p. 51)*.

At the Chavin site of Cerro Sechin there are signs of contact with Olmec and beyond with Ramessid Egypt. The temple platform has the same curvature at the corners *(Kubler, G. 1962, fig. 80)* as the temple of Rameses III at Medinat Habu *(Smith, S.: 1958, fig. 72)*, and the gateway has a pair of salients giving it a fortified appearance for which there are no precedents in Peru. As for the monolithic reliefs at Cerro Sechin they have been compared with "the Danzante" reliefs at Monte Alban in Mexico *(Romero Emilio: 1967, pp. 285-90)*. But the comparison is more than just stylistic. I have shown that the Monte Alban reliefs portray the Ramessid custom of truncating the penises of enemies (above p.33), and in one case at Cerro Sechin the instrument of castration can be seen against the loins and the blood flowing *(Keleman, P.: 1969, I, pl. 99a)*. Again at Huaraz the priest holds the trophy in one hand with an Olmec cross in the other *(Larco Hoyle, R.: 1966, pl. 167)*. I will not dwell here on identities of artifact between Olmec and Chavin, which include types of figurines and pottery, for they have been studied by others *(bibliography in Willey, G.: 1971, p. 288)*.

Instead I shall point to an interesting type of oracular statue found in both areas. The Olmec example is carved in the form of a jaguar god's head. It has a hole going in from the mouth, turning a right angle and, and coming out at the back as if it were "used in a ceremony to make the altar talk" *(Covarrubias: n.d., p. 90)*. The Peruvian example comes from the Ayacucho area. The human statue has a depression in its back large enough to conceal a man, and a hollow tube extends from the mouth to the back of the statue *(Patterson, T.C.: 1971, p. 46)*. This idea survived right up to the time of the Incas who had a statue in the valley of Rimac which spoke and gave answers to questions *(Garcillaso de la Vega in Tomas, A.: 1971, p. 158)*. Compare this with the portable god in Ramessid Egypt who was asked questions and who replied by nodding his head *(Pritchard, J.B.: 1955, p. 448)*.

The Egyptian migrants must have brought this god with them, since we learn from Sahagun that the ancestors who came across the seas carried their god on their backs and "the god went advising them" *(Sahagun: 1950-63, Bk.10, p. 191)*.

In view of all the features shared by the two Formative American cultures and New Kingdom Egypt, still other traits that have been pointed out in a sceptical manner *(Rowe, J.H.: 1966, pp. 334-7)* could now be regarded as legacies brought very probably by the same migrants. These include the horizontal loom staked on the ground, the vertical-frame loom with two warp threads, the T-form axe, and the equal arm balance with pans hung from holes in beam ends.

In view also of the many Egyptian traits in early Peru, it is legitimate to expect to find some evidence that mummification was one of these, as it was in Mexico (see above p.82). Certainly the removal of the viscera from the body *(Elliot Smith, G.: 1929, pp. 112-3)*, and the skilful embalming to preserve the body sometimes in an excellent state is reminiscent of Egyptian practice. Bodies were not only sun dried, but were in some instances treated with preservatives as in the case of the primitive fishermen at Arica on the Peruvian Coast *(Nordenskiold, E.: 1931, pp. 22, 28, 48)*. According to a Chinese source of 1584 the Peruvians smeared balsam oil extracted from trees to preserve the corpse *(Goodrich, L.C.: 1938, pp. 400-411)*. Moreover the practice of mummifying animals is found nowhere else than in Egypt and Peru. *(Moodie, R.L.: 1931, p.63, also see p. 20)*. The question of any physical kinship will be resolved conclusively once the shredded tissues of mummies are examined for their type of antigens, a technique very recently developed *(Stastny, P.: 1972)*. But it is no use looking at the mummies of relatively recent origin, as has been done. At any rate the burial of bodies on their back and the use of sarcophagi at Viru *(Larco Hoyle, R.: 1966, p.78)* are further pointers to alien practice. And the fact that the Inca rulers preserved their viscera in golden receptacles in a special temple *(Dixon, R.B.: 1928, pp. 217-8)*, surely recalls the Egyptian practice of preserving the viscera in Canopic jars.

The migrants had never forgotten the promise that on achieving their goal they would be elevated to the stars of the sky. I maintain that on the plain of Nazca they enacted this in a dramatic way. They pictured the sky on earth, and thereby by sympathetic magic they imagined that they had been elevated to it. Ever since their finding in 1941, the lines have been one

91. Gigantic zoomorphic figures outlined on the Nazca desert, Peru. Interpreted as the apotheosis of inhabitants into star constellations.

92. Constellations pictured in human and animal form in New Kingdom tomb. Includes prototype of Tezcatlipoca. (See above Part 6).

of the major puzzles of South American archaeology. According to recent investigations the lines show no deliberate alignments with the heavenly bodies, nor are they calendric, nor associated with burials. And since the representational figures were so large as to be scarcely visible to a man on the ground, it was suggested that they were signals to the gods *(Hawkins, Gerald S.: 1969)*. Capitalizing on the uncertain state of knowledge others claimed that the dead straight lines were marks left by ancient space vehicles. My solution is that the dead straight lines are simulated tracks of the stars across the sky, and the zoomorphic shapes are constellations in the form of animals including bird, spider, monkey, cat, and a lizard (crocodile?) 200 metres long (Ill. 91). What, it might be asked, is the evidence that in Peruvian belief the zoomorphs were connected with stars? The answer to this is found in Acosta. He says that the Incas adored stars and had names for them; and that every beast or bird on earth had its type in the heavens presiding over its increase and welfare *(Hist. Moral de Indias, in Markham: 1869-71, I, p. 176n.)*. Where did this idea of conceiving the constellations in zoomorphic form come from? Again from New Kingdom Egypt where the constellations were depicted in this way (Ill. 92), and in no other contemporary ancient culture as far as is known. Naturally the animals are native ones known to each land. Moreover the incarnation into animals is again an idea of Egyptian origin. The *Book of the Dead* describes the entrance of human souls into hawks, lapwings, swallows, serpents, crocodiles, lotus plants and so on *(Bodenheimer, F.S.: 1960, p. 125)*.

It is awe-inspiring to witness the strength of Egyptian religion leading men to brave great dangers, and to journey to the unknown confines of the world in order to realize the promised bliss.

Postscript 1

Descent from the sky

An immense figure 820 feet long, said to be in white phosphorescent blocks, is laid out on the slope of hills dipping down to the Bay of Pisco in Peru. I believe that it has a different meaning from the Nazca markings which lie a hundred miles away. Two features are particularly noteworthy: one that it does not stretch right down to the ground level but stops well short, and the other that a long rope was found on it *(Von Daniken, E.: 1968, p. 119)*. The implication would seem to be of a great god rising or descending from the sky on a rope. This conception recalls the Egyptian *Coffin Text:* "The great god lives fixed in the middle of the sky upon his support; the guide ropes are adjusted for that great hidden one, the dweller in the city" *(Clark, R.T.R.: 1959, p. 59)*. An Egyptian relief at the Metropolitan Museum seems to depict this exactly (Ill. 93). There are also the texts which speak of the Pharaoh ascending to the sky on a rope or wooden ladder *(Breasted, J.H.: 1912, pp. 110f., 279)*. In the Mexican

94. Codex picture of Quetzalcoatl in his manifestation of the wind god Ehecatl descending to the earth from a rent in the sky by means of a rope.

93. God suspended in the air, and holding rope from the sky on an Egyptian relief.

book, *Codex Vindobonensis,* the god Quetzalcoatl is shown descending to the earth through a hole in the sky holding a rope (Ill. 94). Once again the pattern of myth is from Egypt to Mexico and Peru, and there are no precise parallels in the literature or art of other ancient lands.

Postscript 2

Initial Horizon in Peru

It is possible that one of the reasons the Chavin civilisation is not a replica of Olmec or its parent Egypt, is that Peruvian developments were already in advance of Mexico in certain respects — particularly in architecture and metalwork. Nowhere in the New World were there architectural complexes remotely as old. Those at Chaquitanto *(El Paraiso),* about 15 miles N.W. of Lima, date from c.1600 B.C. *(Engnel, F.: 1966, p. 43f.).* And we now know that gold was being produced by 1500 B.C. In a burial at Waywaka gold foil and gold working tools were found, as well as lapis lazuli beads *(Grossman, J.W.: 1972, p. 270f.).* It is to say the least strange that other traits of civilisation are not found at the time such as dense population, social complexity, elaborate internal communications and ideas. The absence of all these had been admitted *(Bushnell, G.: 1971, p. 250).*

Could the abrupt appearance of new material traits in Early Formative or the Initial Horizon in Peru be explained by contact with one of the high civilisations of the Old World? This possibility should be entertained. For example because the gold at Waywaka was associated with lapis lazuli, it could be significant that large quantities of lapis lazuli were being exported from Babylonia to Egypt at the time *(Leemans, W.F.: 1960, p. 124, n.3)*. Then there are other possible links between Babylonia and Peru. The wall of conical adobes in the huaca of Pukuche whose circular bases formed a pattern of roundels *(Larco Hoyle, R.: 1941)* recall the clay cone mosaics of Mesopotamia. The divination from entrails practised in Peru ultimately have the same origins, though it has been argued that it was introduced in Peru from late Chou China *(770-256 B.C.) (Obayashi, T.: 1959)*. The modelled head vase excavated on a terrace overlooking the sea at Pacatnamu gave the impression to the excavators of an Assyrian king *(Ubbelohde-Doering, H.: 1966)*. But though apparently found in a late Mochica context (6th-7th Century A.D.), the treatment of the beard recalls to me the bronze head of Hammurabi from Larsa *(Moortgat, A.: 1967, pl. 218)*.

With these few scattered evidences garnered at second hand, I bide my time till the spade has revealed more.

PART 9

The Egyptian Haven at Titicaca

On the southern shores of Lake Titicaca lie the megalithic ruins of Tihuanaco. Because of the scattering of its stones and disturbance of soil in later times, the dating of the complex has given rise to fantastic speculation. A scholar who devoted most of his life to its close study and published massive volumes on it, claimed that it dated back to c.15450 B.C. on the basis of astronomical calculations *(Posnansky, A.: 1945, II, fig.28)*. On the other hand as recently as 1971 a French anthropologist in a responsible position attributed it to Viking activity, and Christian influence of the 13th Century A.D. *(Mahieu, Jacques de: 1971, p. 164)*. The sober judgement of the 'safe' archaeologists is that the monuments date from the Late Formative (after 500 B.C.) to the Classic *(Kubler, G.: 1962)*. With this conclusion I am in closer agreement, though the pointers that ensue will indicate a date still earlier in the Formative Horizon. Clearly the buildings have an affinity with Chavin civilisation which seems to have arisen in the 9th Century B.C. They are also comparable in their magnitude and complexity, and in such details as the post-and- infill wall enclosure which is found in Cerro Sechin *(Kubler, G.: 1962, pp. 304,306)*. The Temple of Tihuanaco also shares with Chavin de Huantar its semi-subterranean nature, corbelled heads dowelled into its exterior wall, and the image of the Staff god.

It could be that the first phase of Tihuanaco is somewhat earlier than Chavin de Huantar, since the conception of the whole and some details as well still bear a traceable relation with Egypt. Although recent Radio carbon dates for the Kalasasaya temple average out at 237 B.C., a few dates are considerably earlier *(Ponce Sanguines, C.: 1972, Table 1)*. I have shown in the previous chapter that the Egypto-Olmec migrants left Mexico and continued their search for Paradise, leaving traces of their wandering in the intermediate lands, till finally they reached Peru and became an element of the Chavin Dynasty there. I now propose to show the resemblances of Tihuanaco with Egypt, and shall close by attempting to explain why this remote site was chosen for one of the great building complexes of the ancient world.

The Kalasasaya Temple at Tihuanaco must have presented a generally similar appearance to the Temple of Seti at Abydos. The latter was described in an inscription as having a lake in front of it like the sea, with papyrus and reeds and lotus flowers in its middle, and its doors were gilt *(Otto, E.: 1968, p. 56)*. All these features were present at Tihuanaco. Though the site of Tihuanaco is now 34 metres above the Lake Titicaca, its docks are stated to have reached the site in ancient times *(Posnansky, A.: 1957, III, p. 192)*. There was also an artificial lake on the surface of the pukara Akapana, or the fortress *(Posnansky, A.: 1945, II, p. 99)*. Similarly there was a pool in the outer temple area at Medinat Habu, as also in the Temple Palace of Merenptah *(University of Chicago: 1953, pt. 1, pp. 66-68)*. The presence of reeds is suggested by the likelihood that the huge andesite blocks at Tihuanaco were brought there on rafts probably of tortora reeds or possibly of balsa wood *(Ponce Sanguines, C.: 1970)*. Similarly at the site of Puma Punku half a mile away there was a pier or wharf in the centre of the east-west axis of its platform where gigantic tortora rafts must have unloaded their burden *(Posnansky, A.: 1955, II, p. 156)*. In New Kingdom Egypt ships brought granite blocks from Assuan to Luxor, some of which must have weighed nearly 1000 tons *(Clarke, S.: and Engelbach, R.: 1930, p. 34)*. Finally the resemblance extends to gold work on the entrance doors. At Puma Punku some of the gold nails still exist to prove that the door had plates overlaid with gold. *(Posnansky, A.: 1945, II, p. 141)*. Compare this with the inscriptions of Amenhotep III which state that the portals of the Temple of Amon were of gold *(Breasted, J.H.: 1906-7, II, p. 361)* and that of Rameses III (c.1187 B.C.) at Medinat Habu, again for Amon-Re, "like unto the great palace of the horizon whose door posts were of fine gold" *(Ibid, IV, p. 9)*.

The native Indians still call the immense monolithic gateway at Tihuanaco "Inti-Punku" or Sun door *(Posnansky, A.: 1945, II, p. 37)*. Two holes below were intended for setting the door on its base. I believe that not only was the golden door of the sun remembered by the migrants, but also its original symbolic function. In Egyptian conception there was "an open door of the sky" through which the setting sun entered the Underworld, and at Medinat Habu the solar boat is making its way toward the open door. New Kingdom texts extoll the sun for being the guide and "opening up the double doors of the desert region" (the netherworld) (see p. 69). Another text describes how "I reach this land of the glorified and enter in at the splendid portal" *(Erman A.: p. 343)*.

Some Americanists are inclined to attribute the carvings on the Sun Gate to a late period after 300 A.D. presumably because the sculpture and pottery of Tihuanaco have been dated by Radiocarbon to this period *(Kubler, G.: 1962, p. 304)*. In my view if not the sculpture itself then at least its iconography goes back to the earliest phase since it can best be explained by Egyptian mythology. The central figure of "the staff god" has his correlate at Chavin de Huantar, and I have argued their descent from the Egyptian priest holding a pair of staffs each surmounted by a god *(cf. Ill. 89)*. The running winged figures on either side (Ill. 95) are also possibly explained by Egyptian analogy. Pharaohs are depicted running with the ship's tackle, including Rameses III *(University of Chicago: V, pt. 1, pl. 257)*. Moreover the sun god Amon was described as a "runner, racer, courser" *(Pritchard, J.B.: 1955, p. 368)*. I believe that the winged figures on the Sun Door are the elect souls, those who brought the sun's ship to the West, and were then raised to the status of stars,

a conception which I have already elaborated *(above p.83)*. *The Book of Gates* explains that the "never vanishing stars become the rowers of the sun by day" *(Muller, Max W.: p. 26)*. The central figure weeps tears, and this relates him to the weeping sun god of Middle America, who once again originates in Egypt *(above p.65)*. The flanking figures also weep; hence should they not be ministrants of the sun god? One more solar symbol on the Sun Gate is the so-called "Staircase Sign" under the feet of the principal image *(Posnansky, A.:1957, III, pl.VIIIa. pp 17,18)*. It is again of Egyptian origin, for there are Egyptian representations of the sun god seated on top of the isolated stair *(Muller, Max W.: p. 35, fig. 20)* and sometimes this staircase rests on the solar boat in the Underworld (Ill. 96) *(from The Book of the dead of the priestess Anhai, 20th Dynasty)*.

96. Representation of the solar boat with staircase, and twin serpents controlling steering oars in the Egyptian Underworld Iaru or Yaru.

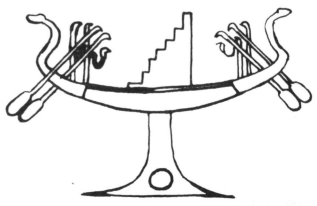

94

Among the reliefs on the Sun Door is a trumpet player in the act of blowing his trumpet while holding a trophy head in one hand *(Posnansky, A.: 1945, I, pl. XXIX.3; II, p.13)* (Ill. 97) as though proclaiming the triumph of the sungod over his enemies. One author has actually claimed that the inspiration for the trumpet player is *The Book of Revelations (VII,1 and VIII,7-13)* of the New Testament, because this type of instrument was never employed in PreColumbian America *(Mahieu, Jacques de: 1971, p. 164)*. This is by no means correct since trumpets dating from the early Centuries A.D. have been found at Teotihuacan in Mexico (also a terracotta figure playing the trumpet), in Colombia (one in gold), and one in Peru itself of the Mochica period c.400 A.D. *(Marti, S.: 1971, pp. 41, 49, 145, 152)*. And as far as is known to me the only older representation of trumpet players in the Old World are in Pharaonic Egypt (Ill. 98), and in Classical Greece.

98. Egyptian trumpeter from Thebes with instrument like the famous trumpet from the tomb of Tutankhamun.

97. Relief of trumpeter holding trophy head (enemies of the sun god?) from Sun Door, Tihuanaco.

It has been claimed that the reverse side of the Sun's Door is the true side of the entrance to the Temple of Kalasasaya *(Posnansky, A.: 1945, II, p. 38)*. And it is on this side that one sees a remarkable parallel with the pylons of New Kingdom Egypt, which again is found nowhere else. Toward the top are pairs of rectangular niches on either side of the portal (Ill.99). This is just what one finds in the Funerary Temple of Rameses III at Medinat Habu, though the upper part of it is rather damaged. *(University of Chicago: 1953, pt.1, pl. 11)*. The pylon of Rameses IV at Karnak has the same feature, and it is intact (Ill. 100). It is clear from the representations of pylons on reliefs that the four niches contained

99. Elevation of the monolithic Sun's Door, Tihuanaco. Reliefs are on the reverse side. Two blind niches are below and four above.

100. Pylon (Gate) of Rameses IV at Karnak from an old photo.

96

brackets which served to support four flag poles that adorned the entrance to the temple *(Otto, E.: 1968, pl. 33)*. The function of the four niches in the Sun Door at Tihuanaco do not appear to have been the same, because the larger niches below were not for holding posts, but they may just be vestigial.

I shall now show a further sequence of techniques and features at Tihuanaco which have Egyptian antecedents. If Posnansky is right, the Sun Door was intended as the centre of a gigantic Calendrical Wall containing hieroglyphs and "ideasymbolic" inscriptions *(Posnansky, A.: 1945, II, pp. 37, 43, 245, fig. 28)*. I know of no closer parallel than the Mortuary Temple of Rameses III at Medinat Habu, where the whole of the outer face of the South wall consists of a great Calendar Inscription. It is in fact the most complete temple calendar surviving, and it lists 35 annual feasts beginning with New Year's Day *(University of Chicago: III, pl. 131f.)*.

Another influence of Medinat Habu would appear to be the heads dowelled into the facade of the Temple of Kalasasaya, a feature which also appears at Chavin de Huantar. In the Funerary Temple of Rameses sculptured heads of foreign prisoners are used as consoles on the Eastern fortified Gate and in the Window of Royal Appearances *(University of Chicago: 1953 etc., Pt.1, p.40, fig. 18; pls. 3 and 33G)*.

An architectural feature found only at Tihuanaco and nowhere else as far as I know in the New World is the clamp or coupling. I-form depressions in masonry blocks had bronze or copper bolts (Ill. 101a). They are suggested to have served to repair the wall of former periods *(Posnansky, A.: 1945, II, p.56)*. It still remains to be ascertained that the clamps were used in the earliest phase of Tihuanaco. If this is so then again Medinat Habu could be the prototype, for here the stone blocks were connected with dovetails which were probably of wood, lead, copper or even of stone (Ill. 101b). They are thought to have been used to keep one block against another while the mortar was setting, whereafter they were removed and reused. *(Clarke, S. and Engelbach, R.: 1930, p. 113)*.

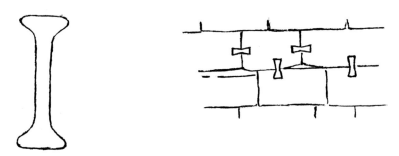

101a. Masonry at Tihuanaco was held by clamps of this form.

101b. Stone blocks held together with dove-tails from Medinat Habu.

Again the actual quarrying method, if correctly described, must have been identical in Egypt and in Tihuanaco. The masonry which was quarried in the volcanic mountain of Kjapphia near Tihuanaco may have been detached from the rock by wedging dry wood in the notches and borings and pouring water on these to make them expand *(Posnansky, A.: 1945, II, p. 231)*. In the granite quarries at Assuan wedge slots for taking the wood are still visible, and their function was the same *(Clarke, S. and Engelbach, R.: 1930, p. 30)*.

And finally the tall rigid idols found at Tihuanaco (largest standing 7.30 metres) are suggested to have been "real columns" possibly supporting a superstructure like caryatids *(Posnansky, A.: 1945, II, p. 212)*. If this were so then they would have appeared like the great Rameses statues at Medinat Habu. They gave the illusion of support as they stood in front of the north colonnade of the First Court, and in the N.E. corner of the Second Court *(University of Chicago: pt. 1, pls. 15, 39)*.

One of the idols at Tihuanaco is a female and is thought to have represented the goddess of the food-giving earth Pachamama. She has multiple (twenty) braids, and this coiffure has been compared with that of a woman of the almost extinct "Chipaya" Indian tribe *(Posnansky, A.: II, fig. 119, cf.115, III, p. 193)*. To me this recalls a wig worn by the false head attached to a mummy bundle excavated at Ancon. The hair is plaited in some 200 thin tresses made of vegetable fibre dyed black *(Reiss, W. and Stübel, A.: 1886-7, I, pl. 21a)*. And this in turn is just like the wig from Thebes in which clusters of thin plaits were padded with sheep's wool *(British Museum: 1922, p. 264)*.

In closing this chapter, I would like now to answer the question why it was that the Egyptian migrants chose this remote site at a great height of over 12,000 feet above sea level, where even the air is difficult to breathe. It is because they identified this place with the paradise they had been seeking, and this is proved by the Egyptian name Iaru or Yaru. The same name Yaro appears as the Peruvian name for paradise, and it has the same rural conception. In Peruvian belief there was a place in the land of the dead called Yarocaca where there were many fields *(Zuidema 1971: 35-6)*. Who can doubt that the Egyptian Yaru is not the Peruvian Yaro? The *Book of Day* of Rameses IV says: "As to the fields of Yaru, it is the city of Re", the sun god *(Piankoff, A.: 1954, I, p. 402)*.

As I envisage it, the Gate of the Sun at Tihuanaco symbolised the open door of the sky which led to the Underworld abode, the Kalasasaya Temple. But before entering the "Underworld" there had to be a journey by boat from the Island in Lake Titicaca. Archaeological evidence shows that Early Tihuanaco remains are found only on the Island of Titicaca and on the site of Tihuanaco itself, and they are not comparable to any other Peruvian or Bolivian stye *(Bennett, Wendel C.: 1963)*. My conclusion that there were solar boats on Lake Titicaca comes from the later evidence that during the Tihuanaco dominance of the Peruvian coast for the first time the *guaras* with centre boards (and presumably having sails) were buried with the dead *(Lothrop, S.K.: 1964, p. 208)*. The practice of boat burials again has Egyptian antecedents. In the Tomb of Amenhotep II at Thebes were model boats of cedar and sycamore *(Daressy, M.G.: 1902, Nos. 4944-6; pl. XLVIII)*, while in the Tomb of Tutankhamun there was a whole fleet of boats of every form with prows to the West (Desroches-Noblecourt, C.: 1965, p. 60). I claim that there were "solar" boats on Lake Titicaca not only because the sails of reed boats there still have solar symbols on them, but also because the original purpose of the Egyptian journey was a solar voyage. Titicaca never forgot these solar origins. Cieza de Leon c.1540 reports the belief of the Indians that the sun once rose from the Island, and that is why they venerated it and built there a temple to the sun *(Bandelier, A.F.: 1969, p. 237)*. Does this not recall the *Book of the Dead* which says that the sun god Ra himself dwells in the Underworld lake *(Budge, E.A.W.: 1898, III, p. 51)?*

And finally there is the account of the mythological origin of the Incas. According to Father Cristoval de Molina c. 1580 - "The Creator commanded Mango and his brothers and sisters to descend under the earth. They came out again at the cave of Paccari-Tambo, at the point where the sun rose on the first day. Thus they were called the Children of the Sun, and the sun was worshipped and revered as a father". *(Markham, C.R.: 1873, pp. 4-6)*. I see here reminiscences of Rameses III sending his expedition to the Underworld, the migrants looking back toward the sunrise with disappointment, and the consequent further voyage till they reach the haven at Titicaca, where they inherit the title almost exclusive to the Pharaohs of Egypt — "the Son of the Sun". I maintain that the Inca myth had simply been handed down to account for and add prestige to the founder of dynasties, but at the back of it lay a core of substantial fact.

One can only wonder how Egyptian traits had survived so long right up to the Incas (by *quipu* record?) — the golden obelisks, oracular statues, canopic jars, royal titles, solar reed boats, and paradisal lakes.

CHAPTER IIIB
Refugees from China

When the Egyptian and Middle Eastern elements in Olmec culture have been accounted for, there still remain a number of facets whose origins must be sought elsewhere. Look for example at the great stone mother goddess of Monte Alto found on July 17th, 1968 in Guatemala *(Remy, C.: 1970, p. 48)* (Ill. 102). She has her hand on her abdomen and she gazes upward with her flat face. We have to go to Shang China to see another seated, flat-faced sky-ward gazing figure, this time in marble and with incised designs *(Chen Te-k'un 1960, pl. XII)* (Ill. 103). The goddess of Guatemala is evidently a deity of childbirth. And since she is the first in the Americas as far as we know, one thinks of Shang China where childbirth was under the care of the three named ancestresses *(Shih, C.C.: 1964. p. 118)*. Some would say that these resemblances are not enough, and that we need something more to establish the presence of the Chinese.

103. Stone sculpture of Shang Dynasty from China with figure turning head skyward.

102. Stone goddess of Formative Period from Guatemala carved on boulder holdin abdomen and gazing up.

Well, what about the physiognomy of the what I would call phase 2 Olmecs? Don't they have slant eyes puffed and with epicanthus fold typical of the Chinese? The American Indian may have been ultimately Mongoloid, but surely nothing could be more Chinese than the Olmec terracotta head in the Museo Diego Rivera (Ill. 104).

104 Olmec terra-cotta head at Museum of Diego Rivera with Chinese features.

Still not conclusive, you might say, and anyway it just can't be explained how the Chinese could have got here at the time. For as Caso says "there is nothing which would suggest that the Shang people might have undertaken sea voyages, other than along the coast, and transoceanic ones were clearly out of the question for them. Both the Shang and the Chou were a land people and not a sea power". He further argues that had they undertaken long maritime expeditions they could scarcely have failed to touch or affect Japan, Hawaii and the rest of Polynesia on the way to America. *(Caso, A.: 1962, p. 16)*. These are on the face of it convincing objections, and nothing in my investigation of early Chinese marine activities as known through literary texts suggests the use of more than rafts and river boats (See Vol. II). Whatever the literary evidence, we shall see that there is physical evidence of the Chinese among the Olmecs, and hence we have to conclude that a voyage was in fact made, and perhaps the flat-bottomed jade canoe that the Olmecs dedicated *(Bernal, I.: 1969, p. 20)* is a remembrance of the same. With regard to rafts it has been argued that the ancestral forms of the coastal and lake rafts of South America were brought coastwise from Asia by emigrants *(Hornell, J.: 1946, p. 44)*. Be that as it may, we must remember in this context what Confucius had said: "If the way does not prevail, I will get on a raft and drift out to sea". This is precisely what I believe must have transpired when the great Shang dynasty was laid low after many centuries of rule.

The *Shoo King* gives a fragmentary account of this important event *(Medhurst, W.H.: 1846, p. 182f)*. In 1121 B.C. the Chou leader Wu-Wang attacked Chao, the ruler of Shang. But before he did so he accused him of being debauched and of thinking only "of palaces, buildings, terraces, groves, dikes, pools, and extravagant clothes to the neglect and ruin of the people", and he accused him further of "spreading pain and poison over the four seas" *(Ibid, p. 188)*. He exhorted his men to attack like tigers and panthers, bears and hyenas *(Ibid, p. 192)*. On conquering the Shang he respected their intelligent men *(Ibid, p. 194)*. *The Mirror of History* adds that he distinguished the families of the clever men among the enemy who had gone away *(Ibid, p. 369)*. After the conquest the thoroughfares were opened to the nine kinds of foreigners and the eight tribes of barbarians, no matter from how far or near they brought tribute *(Ibid, p. 209)*. The reference to the four seas is of interest, and to the escape of the clever men. If these Shang refugees would have sailed away in large numbers to search for new fortunes (the way not having prevailed) some might have been borne by storms all the way to America. The same Chinese text singles out a great storm in 1115 B.C. with a wind so savage that it tore up trees and flattened grain *(Ibid, p. 214)*. It is curious that in 1114 B.C. the succeeding boy-king reflects on his premature enthronement and exclaims "I feel as if I had to cross a great deep" *(Ibid, p. 216)*.

Notice how close to the above date is the date assigned nowadays to the founding of the Olmec ceremonial centre. Coe says "We are fairly sure that the first Olmecs came to La Venta around 1100 B.C.", and adds "We can only guess from where they came" *(Coe, M.D.: 1968, p. 61)*.

Is it so far-fetched to think that the Shang would have been expelled from their own country and established almost immediately afterwards on the other side of the Ocean? Here is an exact parallel from Medieval times. The Omayyad dynasty of Syria were all but exterminated in the 8th century A.D., and its remaining members migrated and set up a new kingdom at the other extremity of the Mediterranean, in Spain, a few years later. And here is a parallel from China itself. When the Chou ruler was forced by barbarian invasion to flee from his capital in 771 B.C., he re-established his court at Loyang in the East *(Watson, B.: 1964, p. 5)*.

We will see evidence of the Shang setting up a state system on the Gulf of Mexico. At this stage in our knowledge we can only conjecture how they were received by the descendants of the Egypto-Olmecs. Having inter-married with the natives, the latter may be imagined to be already 1/2 or 3/4 Mexican at the time of arrival of the Chinese. Can we see any evidence of the Shang at San Lorenzo at all? Let us examine this possibility.

San Lorenzo is dotted with 20 *lagunas* or artificial water holes. There has also been found a 200 meter long system of stone drains to control the water in the complex of ponds. This is admitted to be "the first system of water-control yet known for the New World" *(Coe, M.D.: 1968, p.79, 85, 87)*. From the Old World two possible analogies suggest themselves. In Egypt we have "the Fields of Peace" in the Underworld which were pictured as having a number of pools and lakes, each of which the deceased visit in turn *(Budge, E.A.W.: 1906, III, pp. 43, 48-9)*. And in China we have the dikes and pools to which the last Shang ruler was addicted, a fact to which I have just had occasion to refer. Both the sewage system and draining channels have been found at the Shang capital of Anyang *(Cheng Te-k'un: 1960, pp. 11, 21; pl. 2a)*. I may also point out how according to traditional reports Yu, the founder of the Hsia dynasty c. 1818 B.C., made water channels to divert the streams into the great rivers when the land was threatened with floods *(de Bary: 1964, I, p.80; cf. also p. 187)*. As for the houses at San Lorenzo, these are only known from the little house mounds which are often arranged on two or three sides of tiny family plazas, and Michael Coe suggests that they are "like the extended family dwellings of Chinese farmers" *(Coe, M.D.: 1968, p.82)*.

Within a few years of living at San Lorenzo, the Shang must have decided to found their own ceremonial capital at La Venta, for it is here that Shang influences are rampant. These are as follows:

The choice of site. La Venta has been truly called the "sanctuary in the swamps" where the typical weather is "grey and drizzly" *(Coe, M.D.: 1968, p. 53)*. The reasons for the choice of such a site is perhaps explicable by referring to the *Book of Feng-Shan*. It says "Since Heaven is disposed to cloudiness or obscurity, the sacrificial place must be chosen below the high mountains, and atop a small hill, which is commonly refered to as 'Chih', while earth becomes precious because of sunshine, therefore sacrifices must be made at a circular mound in a swampy land" *(Ling Shun-Sheng: 1968, p. 187)*.

The layout. La Venta is the earliest site yet known in the Americas to be set apart as a ceremonial centre, and to be orientated to the four directions. This is what the *Chou li* classic has to say about planning a city for the prince Ching Wong in 1108 B.C., very close in date to La Venta itself. "Now when the kings founded the empire they determined the four cardinal points of the compass and fixed the positions ... A space of ground 1000 li square was styled the king's domain". All around the marshy and brushwood ground were guardian hills and water tanks each with their name *(Gingell, W.R.: 1852, p. 1f.)*.

The orientation. The ceremonial centre of La Venta is not orientated exactly to the North, but is deflected 8° to the West of it. That this deflection was not accidental is proved by the contemporary site of Poverty Point in the Lower Mississippi Valley in the United States, and also at Laguna de los Cerros where the mounds are once again placed 8° to the left of the true cardinal direction *(Ford, J.A.: 1969, pp. 46, 191)*.

In China deflections are once again consistent though not quite as precise. According to one source the Shang tombs at Anyang c.1300 B.C., are all orientated from 5° to 12° East of the present true North, which is suggested to be accounted for by precessional change *(Needham, J.: 1962, vol.4, pt.1,pp.312-3)*. Another explanation given is that in 600 B.C. the North was not indicated by the Pole Star but by Ursa Minor which was then revolving round the pole at a distance of 7° from it *(Hansford, S.H.: 1968, p.65)*. Notice that the latest study of the question of orientation at La Venta concludes that Ursa Major must have been used for the alignment of its main axis *(Hatch, M.P.: 1971, pp.1-64)*. No suggestions were made as to where this idea may have come from, but once again Egypt is a distinct possibility since Egyptian texts actually refer to temples being orientated to Ursa Major, "Bull's Thigh" *(Nissen: 1906, p.33)*. Moreover we have already seen close links in the mythology of this constellation in Egypt and in Mexico (see p. 63). The Babylonians at La Venta could not have been consulted about its orientation. They had a different tradition, for all buildings including private houses in Mesopotamia had their corners (and not their sides) roughly orientated to the cardinal points. *(Delougaz, D, et al: 1967 p.278)*.

Nevertheless the Babylonian presence at La Venta seems to be indicated by one of the lesser monuments. It is claimed that one of the smaller pyramids (Al) had a stepped form *(Bernal, I.: 1969, p. 36)*. If this turns out to be so, then it will be the earliest such building in the Americas, and hence an urgent need for excavation. There has been much nonsense written about an Egyptian origin for the Mexican pyramids, and I shall return to the question in an appendix. There we shall see that China received the stepped pyramid direct from Babylonia, but at a date just too late to bring to North America. The many Olmec mounds on the Gulf Coast have not yet been investigated, and one should postpone judgement. According to one author they are of almost every shape except that of the rectangular flat-top pyramid *(Ford, J.A.: 1969, p.15)*. The only Olmec pyramid yet studied in detail - the principal one at La Venta which is nearly 35 metres high — has the form of a fluted cone, and later we shall suggest what was implied by this shape. (see p. 113).

It may be that the Phase I Olmec immigrants had been permitted to decide the shape and symbol in return for their labour and co-operation, and the Phase 2 Olmecs to have carried out the scheme introducing other ideas of their own. The resulting synthesis seemed so original that the monument was declared to be "a pure invention with no antecedents" *(Heizer, R.F.: 1968, p.17, fig. 3, and p. 20; 1968a, vol. 42, pp. 52-6)*.

The Babylonian temple towers were not isolated structures, but were contained within sacred enclosures in which there were also other buildings as at La Venta. In early China also there were complexes, though this topic has largely been neglected. I may point out that immediately upon vanquishing the Shang, the Chou ruler erected in 1119 B.C. three altars with their terraces where the three ancestors were prayed to, and another on the south but facing north *(Medhurst, W.H.: 1846, p.211)*. And again like La Venta, two Shang cities investigated, Cheng Chou and Hsia T'un both had a ceremonial and administrative enclave, while the peasants and artisans lived in villages through the surrounding countryside *(Wheatley, P.: 1970, p.161f.)*. It is possible that the Shang migrants regarded the La Venta mound as a memorial to their ancestors, while the Egypto-Olmecs thought of it as a ritual entrance to the underworld. It is my view that composite ideas arise when dominant interests have to make compromise solutions. From the evidence of archaeology there may have been devastation and destruction in Olmec society c. 900 B.C., but at the time of building La Venta nearly 200 years before there was a pooling of resources, and a consequent mingling of diverse beliefs.

Mosaics are another innovation at La Venta, and no earlier examples are known in the Americas. Three deliberately buried mosaic pavements have been excavated at La Venta — one of them just north of the great mound. They are made up of serpentine blocks set in place in coloured clay. Though highly conventionalised they undoubtedly represent the Olmec jaguar (Ill. 105). For a prototype of the technique we are once again led back to the Shang capital of Anyang. Here there were excavated tigers on musical stones which had been inlaid and painted with decorative pieces. The pieces had disappeared long ago, but their impression had been left on the stamped earth *(Li Chi: 1957, p.33; pl. V).*

105. Mosaic of serpentine slabs forming schematized jaguar head from La Venta, now at Villahermosa.

Jade carving among the Olmecs is one of the strongest pointers to Chinese origins. It did not matter that the Chinese used nephrites and the Olmecs the much harder and heavier jadeites, for this was a difference in the availability of local materials. Nor did it seem to matter that the Olmecs had no metal tools; they could still carve with great skill and finesse. It is claimed that there are parallels in technique between Chinese and Olmec jade carving: these include cutting with fibres or wooden slats, perforating with bow or pressure drills, and polishing with abrasives and splinters *(Balser, C.: 1968, p.61).* Conceptually also there are later parallels, for example in the use of the word for jade to describe green landscape, for its use in the names of gods and rulers, and in the placing of a piece of jade in the mouth of the dead *(Stirling, M.W.: 1968, p.19f.).*

Celts. These are smooth blade-like objects of stone with a flat cross-section and tapered on the ends. Groups of celts were found buried as offerings in the ceremonial centre at La Venta. The fact that a number of these celts are made of soft serpentine is proof that they could not have been intended as axes. It is therefore better to call them pseudo-celts *(Ford, J.A.: 1969, pp.51, 53)*.

One group of six celts was placed as an offering under the Ceremonial Court together with sixteen human figures of jade or serpentine (Ill.106). This unique little group is undoubtedly intended to portray some sort of ceremonial assembly. The men all have deliberately deformed heads, some are darker than others, and some more Chinese-looking. The leader is in an entirely different material: the others are gathered round him in a semi-

106. Jade cache from La Venta now at Museo Nacional. Assembly of figures and celts.

circle. Another offering of this kind was placed immediately above one of the jaguar mask pavements. Here there were twenty celts arranged along four directions with a concave mirror at the intersection *(Coe, M.D.: 1968, p.63)*. This mirror I shall be showing (see p. 112), was the equipment of the priests. The celts I now identify with the Chinese *kuei* tablets of jade which were of almost identical shape (Ill. 107), though most popularly used by the Chou Dynasty. These sceptres were insignia of power and rank, and served to distinguish the five classes from each other and from the emperor.

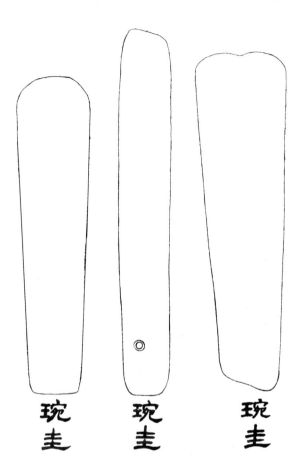

琬 琬 琬
圭 圭 圭

107. Early Chinese celts used as sceptres (Kwei tablets) denoting different ranks of the feudal aristocracy.

The ranks were dukes, marquises, lords, knights and barons, arranged in a kind of feudal aristocracy. The sceptres were held in the hand on the occasion of the four seasonal audiences. "In the spring the *Chau* presentation took place when matters of the empire were discussed; in the autumn there was the *Kin* audience when the meritorious works of the border-officers were compared; in the summer was the *Tsung* levee, at which the different plans proposed through the empire for the benefit of the state were considered; and in the winter there was the court, when the measures or plans of the princes of the empire were harmonized" *(Gingell, W.R.: 1852, pp.33-34)*. The shapes and length of the tablets varied: "the tablet of power" of the Emperor was 14 inches long, and the others were 7 inches long *(Laufer, B.: 1912)*. If this system was indeed introduced among the Olmecs, one would expect some trace of social differentiation to be indicated. An attempt has been made to show that a hierarchy did exist *(Bernal, I.: 1969, p.90)*.

The Jaguar. We have seen that the great bearded giant of the Juxtlahuaca cave wore a lion skin just as Gilgamesh is said to have worn (see p. 26). Such a figure seems to have survived into Aztec times in Duran's description of an ancient man dressed in the skin of a mountain lion who was actually known as Old Mountain Lion *(Duran, Fray D.: 1971, pp.177-8)*. We have also seen that Egyptian priests wore leopard skins over their linen robes (Ill. 12). Finally we have seen that Maya ancestors who came across the sea from the east were called Branches, as was the Egyptian underworld boat which had lion terminals (above p. 11). These may be some of the sources for the Olmec jaguar cult which became such an obsession with them.

There are, however, two particulars in which there are possible links with the tiger cult of China. The first of these, relating to style of representations, has been observed before by Covarrubias *(1966, p.179)*. He points out that the strange (Olmec) concept of disguising and stylising the subject matter until it becomes unrecognisable and turns into abstract decoration is also to be found in Shang and Chou China. I may mention here for example a Shang stone and a jade incised with stylized tigers. *(Cheng Te-k'un: 1966, pp.278a, 300a).*

The second resemblance is that "tiger-like" was a quality aspired to by warriors, and from the evidence I have gathered there appear to have been tiger warriors in China. We had already observed that in defeating the Shang, the Chou general exhorted his men to attack like tigers and other wild animals (above p. 102). After the successful issue of this war c.1120 B.C. the armament was wrapped up in tiger's skin, and stowed away *(Medhurst, W.H.: 1846, p.370)*. Incidentally in the Shang oracle bones there are references to the capture of tigers; this would be in the 14th century B.C. *(Li Chi: 1957, pp.23-4)*. In the Western Chou states there were "tiger warriors", and in an inscription from the reign of King I (934-910 B.C.) they are regarded as the ancestors of a noble who is to inherit from them in the course of an investiture ceremony *(Cho-yun Hsu: 1966, p. 516)*. In c.680 B.C. a chief minister advises duke Huan that in the rites (li) the feudal lords of the higher grade should present leopard skins through emissaries and the lesser lords should present deer skin in return *(Rickett, W.A.: 1965, p.63)*. Duke Hsiao (221-207 B.C.) hoped that by possessing the power of a tiger or a wolf, to be able to swallow up the other feudal lords *(de Bary: 1964, I, p.189)*. In c.100 B.C. Ch'ien Ta-chao claimed that an auspicious jade tablet with the carving of a tiger was used for mobilising troops *(Dubs, H.H.: 1938, I, p.245, n.2)*.

But if the Olmec jaguar cult was initially sparked off by the lion-tiger-leopard cults of Asia and Egypt, it continued to evolve on American soil and developed traits of its own. First the jaguar seems to have been slaughtered ritually, and the cleft on the skull as represented in some Olmec jades is an evidence of this. In fact in one jade carving the engraving shows the jaguar holding a sacrificial knife with which it has cut a V-shaped cleft, such as appears on the second jaguar above it *(Bushnell, G.H.S.: 1965, p. 20)*. Such cleft heads could have been signs that they had been ritually

08. Side of Olmec
one sculpture with
two priests holding
ere-jaguar babies.
ne priest wears
oncave mirror.
illahermosa.

killed, and to wear their masks would in effect confer the power of the jaguar to the wearer through sympathetic magic. In another representation children are wearing such jaguar masks with cleft heads (Ill. 108). They are being carried in the arms of two persons who I believe are shaman priests, for one is wearing a concave mirror. It may be that they are being trained from childhood to cultivate jaguar-like qualities. And alas it may have been this generation of jaguar-men who wrought the first destruction of Olmec society in c. 900 B.C., and vented their savagery on the monuments.

Shamans. Before the coming of the Olmecs there were no male figurines in the highlands of Mexico, and then there appears an interesting figure who could, it is thought, be a combination of a magician and witch doctor *(Bernal, I.: 1969, p.134)*. The terracotta from Tlatilco carries a bundle of rods in one hand and a bulbous object in the other *(Covarrubias, M.: 1966, fig. 6, p. 25)*.

The belief in supernatural spirits together with the ability to control them could have been introduced into Mesoamerica by Shang priests. From the Oracle Bones it appears that the augur-priests could make pronouncements even on political and military affairs *(Watson, W.: 1966, pp. 60-1)*. And it is suggested that they may have been able to induce the ecstatic trance, and to communicate with the world of spirits and ghosts *(Watson, W.: 1961, p. 106)*.

In the 5th century BC. Mo Tzu did some research into the beliefs in spirits and ghosts, and was able to trace it back historically in Chinese society to pre-Shang times. He observes that in Chou times there were references to ghosts and spirits who had sought retribution. One of their kings named Yu set out in the 8th century B.C. to subdue the ruler of Miao. A spirit with the face of a man and the body of a bird came bearing a jade baton to wait on him. He conquered the Miao and "clearly regulated the four extremities of the world so that neither spirits nor people committed any offence, and all the world was at peace" *(Watson, B.: 1967, pp. 56,96f.)*.

There are two distinct proofs that shamanism was brought to the New World. One is that in both areas — in Central and Northern Asia, and in North America, the shamans made use of a tambourine *(Laufer, B.: 1931, pp. 99-101)*. And secondly that most characteristic Chinese form of divination — scapulimancy, is also to be found among the Athabaskan and Algonkian Indians, in the form of divining from markings on shoulder blades *(Cooper, J.M.: 1928, p. 205f)*. Similarly, scrying or seeing visions in a smooth surface of water seems also to have found its way to North America from Asia where it had been prevalent among Semites (Besterman, T.: 1924, p. 72). Jacinto de la Serna confirms that "looking into water" was one of the magic remedies practised in Mexico *(Seler, E.: 1939, II, pt. 1, p.54)*.

There is as yet no evidence that scapulimancy was practiced by the Olmecs. Olmec reliefs have what looks like tortoises on the head of a person, one on a victim at Monte Alban, and possibly one on a warrior or shaman armed with hooked staff on a relief now at the Parque La Venta, Villahermosa (Ill. 109). It is notable that the Shang had replaced the scapula with tortoise shells for their written records and for divining, since the tortoise was an auspicious creature in China.

109. Olmec boulder sculpture now at Villahermosa, with what could be Shaman priest wearing a tortoise on headdress

The shamans continued to be influential in later Mexico. Sahagun, describing Aztec religion, says the sorcerers went about carrying the jaguar hide, and with them they did daring deeds, and because of them they were feared *(Sahagun: 1950-63, bk. 11, p. 3).* The Naguals were "transforming witches" *(Foster, G.M.: 1944, p. 85f.).* Missionaries refer to Indians who had the power to transform themselves into a jaguar, a tiger, an eagle and so on *(Pitt-Rivers, J.: 1970, pp. 198-9).* In Bolivia there are reports of witches changing into jaguars and killing their enemy *(Metraux, A.: 1943).* How this was effected is difficult to say. One imagines there would be autosuggestion, hypnosis, and the medium would have to train to feel, look, and act in a certain way. I believe that among the Olmecs facial distortion was practised so that anyone who belonged to the jaguar clan was readily recognisable. From the drill holes at the corners of the mouth on some jade figures *(Bernal, I.: 1969, pls. 68b, 62; Covarrubias, M.: 1966, pl. XVI),* it would seem that some kind of lip stretchers were used to affect the look of a jaguar. But the grown-up could not readily cultivate this look, and just like cranial distortion it had to be practised from childhood, and one could dedicate one's child to the jaguar cult. This is probably the explanation for the were-jaguar babies cradled in the arms of their normal fathers (Ill. 110).

110. Olmec statue in greenstone from Las Limas (now in Museum of Vera Cruz) Priest incised with symbols of gods, holding jaguar baby having two St. Andrew's crosses on front.

The Olmec shamans had as one of the tricks of their trade, a concave mirror, hung round their necks, so that when the initiate looked in this mirror his facial distortion became even more pronounced. Not only have we seen the representation of a shaman wearing such a mirror, but superbly ground concave mirrors have actually been excavated *(Coe, M.D.: 1968, p. 63)*. Both for the shape of the mirror and for the use of such a mirror in ritual there are Asiatic analogies. Bronze mirrors of the Chou dynasty were round, and were either flat or slightly convex or concave. They had loops at the back for suspension *(Cheng Te-K'un: 1963, pp. 249-50)*. There is an inscription on a mirror ascribed to the Chou founder Wu-Wang (1122-1116 B.C.) which reads: "Think what is behind you, while looking at what is before you" *(Hirth, F.: 1907, p.234)*. The interpretation of this rather obscure statement is liable to vary, but in the Japanese *Nihongi Chronicle,* there is a mention in the part describing events before the 8th century B.C. of gods being produced from two white-copper mirrors *(Aston, W.G.: 1896, I, p. 20)*. And again, in the same text, the first chief priest is said to have been made divine by means of the Greater Divination (i.e. Scapulimancy). Immediately after this it is stated that "at this time a person took in her hand the precious mirror, and giving to another said: "My child, when you look on this mirror, let it be as if you were looking on me . . . let it be to you a holy mirror" *(Aston, W.G.: 1896, I, pp. 82-3)*. These may be the ancestral roots from which transformation witches of America ultimately developed. Much more work needs to be done on these topics by searching through ancient literature. Had the books on invisibility and magic brought to Japan in 602 A.D. survived *(Ibid, II, p. 126)*, we may have learned something more.

Conclusion. The traits brought by the Chinese to Olmec Mexico were not as abundant or as pervasive as those that preceded and came from across the Atlantic. Nevertheless they extended into every area of life. Not only can we perceive the actual physical presence of the Chinese, but ideas of settlement and planning and artistic techniques like mosaic and jade working. We can also see social and political ideas like hierarchy and ceremonial assemblies and ideas of militarism, magic and religion. In the next volume we shall discover that the Chinese were to come again, and bring quite other things with them.

APPENDIX

Pyramid and Mound.

The Olmec "pyramid" of La Venta is the earliest monumental mound in the Americas. It is, therefore, of great significance in the architectural development of such structures in the Americas. With Egyptians, Babylonians and Chinese forming the core of the Olmec society as we have seen, such a structure was inevitable. What ideas could have gone into its making, and how did it differ from them all? I will attempt a conjectural answer, and then refer to later developments over a wide area.

When the mound of La Venta was cleared of vegetation in 1967 it was found to have the form of a fluted cone (Ill. 111). Heizer suggested it was intended as a surrogate for a volcano with the undulations emulating erosional gullies *(Heizer, R.F.: 1968 (a), pp. 52-6)*. As we have seen, the Egypto-Olmecs were obsessed by the crater of the volcano St. Martin Pajapan which they imagined to be the entrance into the underworld (see p. 68). They had in fact set out to discover the mountain in the Far West of the world. It is therefore not surprising that the form of the La Venta mound resembles the compact undulating mountain painted in plan in a Ramessid tomb (Ill. 112). Significantly this mountain lies in front of the goddess of the West whom the deceased, now one of the westerners, is in the act of worshipping. The mound has been described as the "portal through which the declining sun passes" *(Davies, N. de: 1927, p. 98, pls. XIII, XIV)*. The La Venta mound may have had the very same implication since jaguar pavements were buried inside, the jaguar being the god of the night-sun, Tepeyollotl.

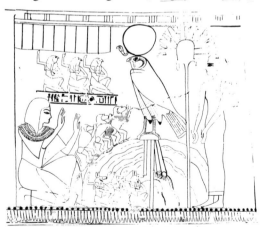

112 Undulating contours of the mountain of the Far West with the solar eagle (cf,ill. 65) and the Western goddess from a Ramessid tomb.

111. Sketch of La Venta mound with its flat top and deliberately undulating exterior.

The next stages in the development of Mesoamerican mounds are necessarily conjectural. It may be that because the sun was imagined to go down into the mound, and before that into the St. Martin crater (above p. 68), it was also conceived of as the place of fire. The mound of Cuicuilco in the Valley of Mexico has circular stages with a stair ramp and a cratered top. The earliest known image of a fire god was found at Cuicuilco. The circular brazier resting on top of the fire god's head could be a survival of the volcanic crater. It may be that the worship of volcanoes was given up after the destructive eruption of the Xitle volcano which almost buried the Cuicuilco pyramid in a lava field, and the god was regarded henceforth as the fire god in the form of a bent old man.

Although the numerous Gulf Coast mounds have not been excavated, one author claims that they are of almost every shape but that of a rectangular flat-top pyramid. There are said to be flat-topped L-shaped mounds, steep cones with pointed peaks, and elongated mounds with long ridge tops *(Ford, J.A.: 1969, pp. 15, 17)*. Up to the present time, the earliest known stepped mound is the 11 metres high Mound 30a at Izapa, which is judged to have been built c.700-600 B.C. *(Ekholm, S.M.: 1969)*. Then comes the Mound I at Tlapacoya of c.500 B.C. in the Valley of Mexico. But it is a stepped platform only 2.6 metres high *(Armillas, P.: 1964, p. 301)*. The mound platform with staircase and six stages at Kaminaljuyu in Guatemala is also early, but its precise chronology is not too clear *(Sandars, W.T. and Michels, J.W.: 1969, p. 82)*.

It used to be argued that the pyramids of Mexico were influenced by those of Egypt. The comparisons and points in common claimed are so superficial and inexact that I need not trouble to refute them here *(Garcia y Cubas: 1871; summary Bancroft, H.H.: 1876, IV, p. 543, n. 89)*.

The question was revived in more recent times, and this time comparisons were made in the methods of construction *(Dupuy, D.: 1939, p. 336)*. But now that we can take the history of pyramids a thousand years further back in Mesoamerica than Teotihuacan, it is obsolete to make comparisons with the latter. In any case, the Egyptian pyramid *(mer)* was a purely funerary structure cut off from the life of the world by being removed to the West bank of the Nile, and away from habitation and cities. And although it had no staircase, it was described symbolically in the texts as a staircase for the kings to ascend to the sun *(Edwards, I.E.S.: 1952, p. 234)*. This conception was taken literally in Mesoamerica where the sacrificial victim ascended to the summit of the pyramid thus imitating the sun's course, according to Duran. He too achieved the sun by having his heart offered to the sun *(Duran: 1971, pp. 188-89)*. Duran *(1971, p. 257)* further claims that at Cholula the pyramid was built "in order to climb to the heavens".

In my view, the Mesoamerican pyramid has, at the root of it, two further traditions — the Babylonian ziggurat and the Chinese tumulus. The ziggurat was at its inception just a temple on a terrace, but it is thought perhaps as a result of reemploying older platforms in rebuilding, the idea of the staged tower may have arisen. And the stages gradually increased in number; the ziggurat of Ur was 4-staged, that of Tchoga Zambil 5-staged, while the tower of Babel was 7-staged *(Busink, T.A.: 1969-70, p. 91f.)*. Nevertheless the conception of the ziggurat as a mountain arose quite early. The Temple of Enlil at Nippur was known as *E-kur*, "the Mountain House" *(Jastrow, M.: 1898, p. 52f.)*, while later Assur's Temple in Assyria was called "the house of the great mountain of the land" *(Dhorme, E.: 1949, p. 73)*. Nabopolassar I's (625-604 B.C.) remark is instructive. He says that he made the Temple of Etemenanki of Babylon "as high as a mountain, and erected it for men to behold" *(Langdon, S.H.: 1905, p. 53)*.

Now I shall show how some very specific ideas connected with the ziggurat were carried to the Far East and beyond. On the summit of the ziggurats was a shrine. Tiglathpileser I (1120-1100 BC.) says he located the gods in this, and prayed to them for, "abundant rain, years of prosperity and fruitfulness in plenty" *(Harper, R.F.: 1901, pp. 25-63.)* Herodotus reports, and texts confirm, that the chamber on top of the tower was a house of joy, where the god, represented by the king, made love to a priestess, thereby promoting the fertility of the city *(Smith, S.: 1928, pp. 849f.)*. This very idea seems to have somehow drifted to Cambodia where it survived as late as the end of the 13th century A.D. A Chinese visitor relates that the King of Cambodia went high up into the tower of the royal temple, and cohabited with the naga princess, and on this union depended the welfare, and even the existence of the kingdom *(Briggs, L.P.: 1951, p. 14)*. As for the shrine on the Babylonian ziggurat, the *gigunu*, it was some times covered in greenery. This was so in the case of the temple of Ai, wife of the Sun god, in the time of Hammurabi *(Smith, S.: 1928)*. And here is a remarkable parallel. Duran *(1964, p.111)* reports that an arbour of branches and leaves of a tree called *tzapotl* had been erected on the summit of the Aztec pyramid . Mexican and Babylonian ideas were once compared, and it was concluded that there was no transmission of religious or astronomical concepts, only that both developed from the same cultural type *(Danzel, T.W.: 1921, p. 243f.)*. The evidence I have accumulated (above p. 22 f.) has proved this to be wrong.

Surprisingly there is even evidence for the ziggurat being taken to China in the 10th century B.C. According to a Chinese account: during the time of King Mu (who had made an expedition to the west in 985 B.C.) a magician, (or priest) came from a country in the remote west . . . King Mu began to use him to build new constructions . . . the *tai* was finally completed, which was 1000 *jen* of height" *(Ling Shun-Sheng: 1965)*. Later in the 4th century B.C. Chu Yuan asks: "Where is Kun lun with its Hanging Gardens? How many miles high are its ninefold walls?Kun lun is argued to be a transliteration of ziggurat, and the reference is to the famous Hanging Gardens of Babylon built by Nebuchadnezzar (605-562 B.C.) *(Ibid, pp. 47-48)*.

According to a Chinese scholar, the *tai* structures of ancient China not only served as praying places, but had other functions. For example they were used for far-seeing purposes, and for giving military instruction

(Ibid, p. 41). Compare what Duran says about the uses of the Aztec pyramid. He says that it was used as a military watch post, and as a platform for addressing soldiers *(Duran: 1964, pp. 158, 187).* When the Chinese and the Mexican pyramids had largely the same form and the same function, may we not allow for the possibility that the Mexican word for pyramid *teo (teocalli)* is related to the Chinese word *tai?* Sahagun, citing his Mexican informant, says that the teocalli "is a place to show" *(Sahagun: 1950-63, Bk. 11, p. 269).* And is this not exactly what Nabopolassar had said about the ziggurat? (See p.115).

Here briefly is what is known about this category of structures in China. Among the earliest surviving is the sacrificial altar of Chou date c.700-500 B.C. at Yang.tzu-shan in Szechwan. The three terraced platforms measure successively about 103, 67, and 31 metres a side *(Cheng Te K'un: 1963, III, pp. 34-6).* Further pyramidal mounds with truncated top of the Chou period are to be found in central Shensi near Hsien-yang. Some are 250 metres square, and some barely 4-5 metres, and they are described as princely graves *(Siren, O.: 1929, pp. 22-26).* Then again there is the triple terraced platform at the Chou city of Hou-ma-Chen It had a ramp on the south side, and the base of a structure at the top *(Wheatley, P.: 1971, p.139).*

In the Han dynasty the stepped pyramid had both uses — as a place of worship and as a place of burial. In 110 B.C. the Emperor Wu performed the *feng* sacrifice on top of Mount T'ai from an altar 120 feet wide and 20 feet high which had three flights of steps to ascend it *(Dubs, H.H.: 1954, II, p. 86, n. 25).* This is known from a literary source, but archaeological evidence confirms it. In one case, near Ch'eng-tu in Western Szechwan the earthen ceremonial platform excavated in 1956 had a height of ten metres. Stairs led across each of the three stages (Ill. 113) *(Kwang-chih Chang:*

113. Stepped altar platform from Szechwan in China.

1963, fig. 21, pp.278-9). In another case at Hsin-t'ien (state of Chin) excavated in 1957, a platform orientated to the four cardinal directions had a sloping ramp going across its three stages to the summit which was 8.5 metres high *(Ibid: pp. 183-5)*. Now truncated stepped pyramids are to be found not only in Mexico (Ill. 114), but in Peru (early Chimu and Tiahuanaco periods), and surprisingly also in Tahiti and Tonga. In both areas the structures are claimed to have been used for worship and for burial, though not everyone will agree with the view that they were taken to the Pacific Islands by Peruvian voyagers *(Heyerdahl, T.: 1952, pp. 396, 402; pls. LVIII, LIX).*

As I have just said, in China the stepped pyramidal form of structure was used not only as an altar but also as a mausoleum. As examples of the latter we have the Han tombs in North Annam *(Janse, B.R.T.: 1947)*, and at Kung-ling where the rulers of the Western Han dynasty (195 B.C. — 5 A.D.) lie buried *(Siren, O.: 1930, p. 7, pl. I)*. The greatest example of course is the tomb of the Ch'in Emperor Shih Huang-ti about 30 kilometres east of Sian-fu *(Siren, O.: 1929, pl. 22c)*. The base line of the pyramid is 340 metres square (as against the 226.5 of the Giza Pyramid of Cheops, and the 225 of Teotihuacan). Ssu-ma Ch'ien says it was begun in 217 B.C., and 70,000 soldiers were employed on it. He describes the room with jewels, the automatic protection devices and symbolic representations, and refers to workmen and the emperor's wives being buried with him. The Han emperor Wen (died 157 B.C.) went to the other extreme. He did not have a mound constructed for reasons of economy, and because "he did not wish to put the people to great labour" *(Watson, B.: 1961, I, p. 362).*

114. So-called Pyramid of the Sun at Teotihuacan whose external measurement nearly equals the Great Pyramid at Giza in Egypt.

It must be understood that the stepped pyramid was only a later form of burial structure in China. The earlier form was the mound. Mo Tzu in the 5th century B.C. says that rulers and officials in his time require a burial mound as round and high as a hill *(Watson, B.: 1967, p. 74)*. But how old is the burial mound in China? According to one author, burial mounds *(kurgans)* appeared in the northern Caucasus (c.2500-2000 B.C.), and spread along the steppes to the Altai mountains. Miniature kurgans reached southern Siberia probably after 1700 B.C., and the full-sized only c.1200-1000 B.C. He claims that burial mounds were first introduced into China by the Chou c.1027. He contradicts himself when he says they may have been slightly earlier (mentioning in passing the imposing tumuli in the Wei River Valley), which would bring us into the Shang period, but he then says that they were not present in the Shang or earlier periods *(Chard, C.S.: 1961, p. 22)*. A Chinese scholar, on the other hand, insists that mounds were in use in late Shang times c.1200 B.C. in the Yangtze delta *(Ling Shun-Sheng 1968)*. According to him, 357 ancient mound sites have been discovered to date. They are burial mounds, circular or oval, with a flat top, and are designated sacred. Some have names after animals like turtle and snake, and are therefore suggested to be reminiscent of the American Indian effigy mounds. A third type are religious or temple mounds with flat tops used for worship or sacrifice and some had temples on them. For example there was a "round mound for the worship of heaven" from the time of the Yellow Lord, founder of the Hsin dynasty, and the emperor Wu (140-88 B.C.) went there regularly to escape the heat *(Dubs, H.H.: 1954, II, p. 91, n. 27.4)*.

All these developments of pyramid and mound must be taken into account when assessing the possible influence on Mexico. It follows from the data presented above that the Shang refugees could have brought the mound idea, but not that of the stepped pyramid, which was introduced in their country of origin after their departure. Therefore, if the stepped pyramid is eventually found in the Olmec Gulf area it may be due to the Semites, who also brought some other Babylonian ideas as we have seen already.

It is a mistake to regard the Mexican pyramids purely as elevated temples. Few people realise that they were also intended as burial places. In 1900 Penafiel said: "It has not been demonstrated that our pyramids were used as sepulchres as in Egypt" *(Penafiel, A.: 1900, p. 31)*. The examples cited by me will establish the case once and for all. In Chiapas at the turn of the era low pyramids contained large tombs with adobe brick walls and timbered roofs *(Ford, J.: 1969, p. 44)*. In the pyramid of Cholula were two skeletons and two basalt idols in a square room whose ceiling was supported by timber beams *(Bancroft, H.H.: 1870, V, pp. 56-7)*. In the pyramid Temple of Quetzalcoatl in Teotihuacan four skeletons were found in the four angles *(Dosal, P.J.: 1925, pp. 216-19)*, and six graves were found on the uppermost terrace together with remains of six big wooden pillars *(Gamio, M.: 1922, p. LXV)*. Sahagun says that in

Teotihuacan the principal men and lords had earthen tumuli built over their graves *(Sahagun: 1950-63, III, p. 141)*. Among the Aztecs we have the testimony of Alonzo de Zorita *(1965, p. 160)* that the 40 high towers in the enclosure of the great temple of Mexico City not only had shrines dedicated to idols, but were places of burials for the lords. Among the Mayas we have the evidence of Landa that the nobles were cremated and their ashes placed in great urns, above which temples were built as at Izamal *(Tozzer: 1941, p. 130)*. And burials have indeed been found in the interior of pyramids, for example at Chichen Itza at the Castillo and the Temple of Warriors, and at Uaxactun *(Tozzer: 1941, p. 131, n. 610)*. In Copan a vault was found on the side of a pyramid in which were pots containing human remains *(Bancroft, H.H.: 1876, V, p. 56)*. In the well-known Temple of Inscriptions at Palenque there is a large vaulted crypt with stone sarcophagus, and it is reached by a stair ramp covered with corbelled vaults. Antecedents exist in the Early Classic Period of Guatemala (300-600 A.D.) where tombmounds have long masonry passage-ways, entrances blocked by stone slabs leading to stone-lined chambers with corbelled vaults, while stone boxes serving as sarcophagi also appear subsequently *(Wauchope, R.: 1965, II, pp. 92-3)*.

The Palenque pyramid with its sloping corbel vaulted gallery leading to a sepulchral chamber undoubtedly recalls the interior of an Egyptian pyramid, but its 6th century A.D. date precludes any direct connections. However we now have galleries leading to corbel-vaulted rooms at a very much earlier date in the pyramid at Totimehuacan, south of Puebla. This

115. Pyramid of the Inscriptions at Palenque which served both as temple and tomb.

is earlier than 200 B.C. and may be as early as the 6th century B.C. *(Spranz, B.: 1970)*. There is also another prototype in the Pyramid of the Moon at Teotihuacan. In 1895 there was found an opening half way up its southern face. This opened into a triple gallery, one of which led to a square pit lined with unburned brick *(Penafiel, A.: 1900, pl. 31-2)*. The Palenque teocalli has an exterior akin to a Babylonian ziggurat (Ill. 115), and an interior to an Egyptian pyramid. In view of my evidence that there were Babylonians and Egyptians in Mexico in Olmec times, this fusion may after all not be coincidence. But then we must also leave room for the influence of Han China. We know from the *Hou Han Shu* that the imperial remains were deposited underneath the mound inside a crypt called *feng* or apartment. This communicated with the outside by a *hung-tung* or "profound cave" closed by a door. And this in turn opened onto the spirit path *shen tao (de Groot, J.J.M.: 1894, II, p. 423)*.

What is needed now is a vast campaign to plot, describe and excavate the numerous Gulf Coast mounds.* This provisional assessment is offered not to anticipate conclusions, but to indicate what intriguing possibilities lie ahead.

---

*A survey of the Gulf Coast mounds is in fact being carried out by the "Projecta Olmeca" of the University of Kansas, but my request for information was ignored.

BIBLIOGRAPHY

Allen, T.G. 1916	*Horus in the Pyramid Texts,* Chicago.
Alonzo de Zorita 1965	*The Lords of New Spain,* tr. B. Keen, London.
Andrews, E.W. 1939	"A group of related sculptures from Yucatan", *Carnegie Institution of Washington,* Publication 509, Contribution 26, Washington.
Antonieta Cervantes, M. 1967	"Dos Elementos de uso rituel en el Arte Olmeca", *Anales,* 1967-68, Mexico, 1, pp.37-51.
Armillas, P. 1964	"Northern Mesoamerica", *Prehistoric Man in the New World,* ed. Norbeck, Chicago.
Aston, W.G. 1896	*Nihongi Chronicles of Japan . . .* 2 vols, London.
Balser, C. 1968	"Metal and jade in lower Central America", *XXXVII Congresso Internacional de Americanistas,* Buenos Aires, IV, pp.57-64.
Bancroft, H.H. 1876	*The Native Races of the Pacific States of North America,* New York, 5 vols.
1883	*Native Races.* San Francisco.
Bandelier, A.F. 1969	*The Islands of Titicaca and Koati,* New York.
Barnett, R.D. 1960	"Some contacts between Greek and Oriental Religions", *Elements Orientaux dans la Religion Grecque Ancienne,* Colloque de Strasbourg, 1958, Paris.
Barton, G.A. 1929	*Royal Inscriptions of Sumer and Akkad,* New Haven.
Baudez, C.-F. 1971	"Commentary on Inventory of some preclassic traits in the Highland and Pacific Guatemala", *Contributions of the University of California Archaeological Research Facility,* vol 11, pp.78-84.
Bennett, Wendel C. 1963	"The Archaeology of the Central Andes", *Handbook of South American Indians,* ed. Steward, J.H., vol.2, New York.
Bernal Diaz 1963	*The Conquest of New Spain,* tr. J.M. Cohen (Penguin).
Bernal, I. 1968	*El Mundo Olmeca,* Mexico.
1969	*The Olmec World,* tr. D. Heyden & F. Horcasitas, Berkeley and Los Angeles.
Bernal, I., and Seuffert, A. 1970	*Yugos de la Coleccion del Museo Nacional de Antropología,* Mexico.
Besterman, T.P. 1924	*Crystal-Gazing,* London.
Blackman, A.M. 1924	"Opening the mouth in Ancient Egypt and Babylonia", *Journal of Egyptian Archaeology,* X, pp.47-59.
—	"The significance of Incense and Libations", *Zeitschrift fur agyptische Sprache und Altertumskunde,* Berlin, Bd.50.
Bodenheimer, F.S. 1960	*Animal and Man in Bible Lands,* London.
Bonomi, J. and Sharpe, S. 1864	*The Alabaster Sarcophagus of Oimenepthah I,* London.

Boreux, C.
1925
Études de Nautique Égyptienne, Cairo.

Borghouts, J.E.
1971
The Magical texts of Papyrus Leiden, Leiden.

Boylan, P.
1922
Thoth the Hermes of Egypt, London, etc.

Bray, D.
1968
Everyday Life of the Aztecs, London.

Breasted, J.H.
1906-7,
1927
Ancient Records of Egypt, Chicago, 5 vols.

1912
The development of Religion and Thought in Ancient Egypt, New York.

1917
"The earliest boats on the Nile", *Journal of Egyptian Archaeology*, IV, pp.174-6 & p.255.

1930
The Edwin Smith Surgical Papyrus, Chicago.

Briggs, L.P.
1951
"The Ancient Khmer Empire", *Transactions of the American Philosophical Soc.*, Vol.41, pt.1.

Brinton, D.G.
1882
American Hero Myths, Philadelphia.

1893
"The Native Calendar of Central America and Mexico", *Proceedings of the American Philosophical Society*. 31, pp.258-314, Philadelphia.

1896
The Myths of the New World, 3rd. edition, Philadelphia.

British Museum
1909
A Guide to the Egyptian Galleries (Sculpture), London.

1922
A Guide to the Fourth, Fifth and Sixth Egyptian Rooms, London.

Budge, E.A.W.
1898, 1901
The Book of the Dead, London.

1899
The Book of the Dead, Facsimiles of the Papyrus of Hunefer, London.

1901
Egyptian Magic, London.

1904
The Gods of the Egyptians, London, 2 vols.

1906
The Egyptian Heaven and Hell, 3 vols., London.

1909
The Book of the Opening of the Mouth, London.

1911
Osiris and the Egyptian Resurrection, London, 2 vols.

1913
The Book of the Dead: The Papyrus of Ani, 2 vols., London.

1926
Cleopatra's Needles and other Egyptian Obelisks, London.

1929
The Book of the Dead, (British Museum Guide), London.

Burland, C.A.
1966
Codex Laud, Graz.

Bushnell, G.H.S.
1965
Ancient Arts of the Americas, London.

1971
"Observations on the Emergence of Civilisation in Meso-America", *Contributions of the University of California Archaeological Research Facility*, No.11, April, Berkeley, Cal.

Busink, T.A.
1969-70
"L'Origine et l'evolution de la ziggurat babylonienne", *Jaar bericht ex Oriente Lux*, No.21, pp.91-142, Leiden.

Carmen Aguilera
1971
"Una posible deidad negroide en el panteon Azteca," *Estudios de Cultura Nahuatl*, 9, pp.47-56.

Carrasco, P.
1971
"The peoples of Central Mexico and their historical traditions", *Handbook of Middle American Indians*, XI, p.460. ed. R. Wauchope, Austin, Texas.

Caso, A.
1947
"The Eagle and the Nopal", *The Social Sciences in Mexico*, I, no.1, May, pp.5-15, Mexico D.F.

1962
"Relaciones entre el Viejo y el Nuevo Mundo", *Cuadernos Americanos*, XXI, 6, pp.1-18.

1964
Interpretacion del Codice Selden, Mexico.

1965
"Existio un Imperio Olmeca?", *Memoria del Colegio Nacional*, Mexico, vol.5, no.3, pp.3-52.

1967
The Aztecs, People of the Sun, Norman, Oklahoma.

122

Casson, L.
1964

Illustrated History of Ships and Boats, New York.

Champollion
1945

Monuments de l'Egypte et de la Nubie, Paris, new ed.

Chard, C.S.
1961

"Invention versus diffusion: the burial mound complex of United States", *Southwestern Journal of Anthropology,* vol.17, pp.21-5.

Cheng Te K'un
1959, 1960, 1963, 1966

Archaeology in China, Cambridge.

Cho-Yun Hsu
1966

"Notes on the Western Chou Government", *Academia Sinica, Bulletin of History and Philology,* XXXVI, pt. 2, Taipei.

Clark, R.T.R.
1959

Myth and Symbol in Ancient Egypt, London.

Clarke, Somers and
Engelbach, R.
1930

Ancient Egyptian Masonry, London.

Clowes, G.S.L.
1959

Sailing Ships, their History and Development, London.

Coe, M.D.
1965

The Jaguar's Children, Preclassic Central Mexico, New York.

1968

"San Lorenzo and the Olmec Civilisation", *Dumbarton Oaks Conference on the Olmec,* ed. E.P. Benson, pp.41-78, Washington, D.C.

1968a

America's First Civilisation, New York.

1970

"The Archaeological Sequence at San Lorenzo Tenochtitlan, Vera Cruz, Mexico", *Contributions of the University of California Archaeological Research Facility,* Berkeley, no.8, 21-34.

Comas, Juan
1972

Hipothesis Transatlanticas sobre el Pablamiento de America, (Instituto de Investigaciones Historicas), Mexico.

1973

"Transatlantic hypothesis on the Peopling of America: Caucasoids and Negroids", *Journal of Human Evolution,* 1973, 2, pp.75-92.

Cooper, J.M.
1928

"Northern Algonkian Scrying and Scapulimancy", *Festschrift P.W. Schmidt,* Wien, pp.205-17.

Cornford, F.M.
1934

The Origin of Attic Comedy, Cambridge.

Covarrubias, M.
n.d.

Mexico South, London etc.

1966

Indian Art of Mexico and Central America, New York.

Danzel, T.W.
1921

"Babylon und Alt Mexico", *El Mexico Antiguo,* I, no.9, pp.243-68.

David, A. Rosalie
1973

Religious Ritual at Abydos, Warminster, Wilts.

Davies, C.H.S.
1894

The Egyptian Book of the Dead, New York, London.

Davies, N. de G.
1927

Two Ramesside Tombs at Thebes, New York.

Davies, N.M.
1936

Ancient Egyptian Paintings, Chicago.

Daressy, M.G.
1897

Notice explicative des ruines de Medinet Habou, Cairo.

1902

Catalogue Général des Antiquités Egyptiennes du Musee du Caire, Fouilles de la Vallee des Rois, Cairo.

1906

Statues de divinités. Catalogue General des Antiquités Egyptiennes du Musée de Caire, Cairo.

de Bary, W.T. ed.
1964

Sources of Chinese Tradition, 3rd printing, New York.

de Groot, J.J.M.
1892, 1894

The Religious System of China, Leyden.

Delougaz, D. *et al.* 1967	*Private Houses and Graves in the Diyala Region,* Chicago.
Description de l'Egypte 1812	published by Napoleon the Great, Paris, vol.III.
Desroches-Noblecourt, C. 1965	*Tutankhamun,* London.
Dhorme, E. 1949	*Les Religions de Babylonie et d'Assyrie,* Paris.
Dixon, R.B. 1928	*The Building of Cultures,* New York, London.
Dosal, P.J. 1925	"Descumbriementos Arqueologicos en el Templo de Quetzalcoatl" *Anales del Museo Nacional de Arqueologia,* Mexico, pp.216-19.
Drucker, P., Heizer, R.F. 1959	"Excavations at La Venta, Tabasco, 1955", *Bureau of American Ethnology Bulletin,* 170, Washington.
Dubs, H.H. 1938, 1954	*The History of the Former Han Dynasty,* Baltimore.
Dupuy, D. 1939	"Les Pirámides del Antiguo y del Nuevo Mondo y la Ciencia de sus Constructores", *Revista Geographica Americana,* Buenos Aires, XII, no.74, pp.325-37.
Duran, Fray D. 1964 1971	*The Aztecs: The History of the Indies of New Spain,* tr. D. Heyden and F. Horcasitas, New York. *Book of the Gods and Rites and Ancient Calendar,* tr. F. Horcasitas and D. Heyden, Norman, Oklahoma.
Easby, E.K. 1966	*Ancient Art of Latin America from the Collection of Jay C. Leff,* Brooklyn Museum, New York.
Edgerton, W.F. and Wilson, J.A. 1936	*Historical Records of Rameses III,* Chicago.
Edwards, I.E.S. 1947	*The Pyramids of Egypt,* London, (reprint 1952).
Ekholm, Susanna, M. 1969	"Mound 30a of Izapa", *Papers of the New World Archaeological Foundation,* no.25, Utah.
Elliot Smith, G. and Dawson, W.R. 1924	*Egyptian Mummies,* London.
Elliot Smith, G. 1929	*The Migrations of Early Culture,* Manchester.
Engnel, F. 1966	"Le Complexe Précéramique d'el Paraiso (Perou)," *Journal de la Société des Américanistes,* Paris, vol. LV-1, pp.43-69.
Erman, A. 1969 (reissue)	*Life in Ancient Egypt,* London, New York.
Estrada, E. and Meggers, B.J. 1962	"A complex of traits of probable Transpacific origin on the Coast of Ecuador", *American Anthropologist,* 63, 1961, pp.913-39.
Fairman, H.W. 1958	*Myth, Ritual and Kingship,* ed. S.H. Hooke.
Feriz, M. 1966	"Sinn und Bedeutung der erotischen Grabbeigaben in Alt-Peruanischen Grabern", *Ethnos,* (Sweden), pp.173-81.
Feuchtwanger, F. 1955	*The Art of Ancient Mexico,* New York.
Field, F.V. 1967	*Thoughts on the meaning and use of Pre-Hispanic Mexican Sellos,* (Dumbarton Oaks), Washington, D.C.
Fischer, H.G. 1968	*Ancient Egyptian representations of Turtles,* Metropolitan Museum, New York.
Flannery, K.V.	*Preliminary Archaeological Investigations in the Valley of Oaxaca, Mexico, 1966-69,* (unpublished report to the National Science Foundation and the INAH, Mexico.

Ford, J.A.   *A Comparison of Formative Cultures in the Americas,* (Smithsonian
1969   Contributions to Anthropology, vol.11), Washington.

Foster, G.M.   "Nagualism in Mexico and Guatemala", *Acta Americana,* 2, (1,2),
1944   pp.85-103.

Frankfort, H.   *Kingship and the Gods,* Chicago.
1948

Frye, R.N.   "Gestures of deference to royalty in Ancient Iran", *Iranica Antiqua,*
1972   Leiden, IX, pp.102-107.

Gamio, M.   *The Population of the Valley of Teotihuacan,* Mexico.
1922

Garcia y Cubas   *Essayo de un Estudio comparativo entre las Pirámide Egipcias y*
1871   *Mexicanas,* Mexico.

Gardiner, A.H.   in *Hastings Encyclopaedia of Religion and Ethics,* VIII, p.21.
1915

1927, 1950   *Egyptian Grammar,* Oxford.
1950   "The baptism of Pharaoh", *Journal of Egyptian Archaeology,* 36,
                    pp.3-12.

Gardiner, J.G.   *A popular account of the Ancient Egyptians,* London.
1890

Gauthier, H.   *Les Fêtes du dieu Min,* Cairo.
1931

Gay, Carlo T.E.   "Oldest Paintings of the New World", *Natural History,* LXXVI, no.4,
1967   April, pp.28-35.
1971   *Chalcacingo,* Graz, Austria.
1972   *Xochipala. The Beginnings of Olmec Art,* Princeton.

Gayet, Al   *Le Temple de Louxor,* Paris.
1894

Gingell, W.R.   *The Ceremonial Usage of the Chinese BC* 1121, London.
1852

Goneim, Mohammed Zakaria
1956   *The Buried Pyramid,* London.

Goodrich, L.C.   "China's first knowledge of the Americas", *The Geographical Review,*
1938   XXVIII, pp.400-11.

Gordon, Cyrus, H.   *Before Columbus,* New York.
1971

Greene, M. *et al* *Maya Sculpture,* Berkeley, California.
1972

Griffith, J.G.   *The Origin of Osiris,* Berlin.
1966

Grossman, J.W.   "An ancient gold workers tool kit, the earliest metal technology in
1972   Peru", *Archaeology,* October, vol.25, no.4, pp.270f.

Guillermo-Lumbreras, L.   "Towards a re-evaluation of Chavin", *Dumbarton Oaks Conference on*
1971   *Chavin,* ed. E.P. Benson, Washington, D.C.

Grove, D.C.   "Chalcatzingo, Morelos, Mexico: a reappraisal of the Olmec rock
1968   carvings", *American Antiquity,* vol.33, no.4, October, pp.486-91.
1970   "The Olmec paintings of Oxtotitlan Cave, Guerrero, Mexico",
                    Dumbarton Oaks Studies in Pre-Columbian Art and Archaeology,
                    no.6, Washington, D.C.

Guitel, G.   "Etude comparée des numerations Aztèque et Égyptienne", *Actes du*
1958   *VIII Congrès International d'Histoire des Sciences,* Florence-Milan,
                    I, pp.52-56.

Hallo, W.W.   "The cultic setting of Sumerian poetry", *Actes de la XVII Rencontre*
1970   *Assyriologique Internationale,* pp.116-34.

Hansford, S.H.   *Chinese Carved Jade,* London.
1968

Harper, R.F.   *Assyrian and Babylonian Literature,* New York.
1901

Hatch, M.P.
1971

"An hypothesis on Olmec astronomy", *Contributions of the University of California Archaeological Research Facility,* no.13, June, pp.1-64.

Hawkes, J.
1962

Man and the Sun, London.

Hawkins, Gerald S.
1969

Ancient Lines in the Peruvian Desert, Smithsonian Institution, Cambridge, Massachusetts.

Hayes, W.C.
1959

The Scepter of Egypt, Cambridge, Massachusetts.

Heizer, R.F.
1967

"Studies in Olmec Archaeology", *Contributions of the University of California Archaeological Research Facility,* no.3, August.

1968

"New Observations on La Venta", *Dumbarton Oaks Conference on the Olmec,* ed. E.P. Benson, Washington, D.C., pp.9-40.

1968a

"The La Venta Fluted Pyramid", *Antiquity,* vol.42, pp.52-6.

1971

"Commentary on 'The Olmec Region—Oaxaca'", *Contributions of the University of California Archaeological Research Facility,* vol.11, pp.51-69.

Helck, W.
1968

Die Ritualszenen auf der Umfassungsmauer Rameses' II in Karnak, 2 vols, Wiesbaden.

Heyerdahl, T.
1952

American Indians in the Pacific, London.

Highbarger, E.L.
1940

The Gates of Dreams, Baltimore.

Hirth, F.
1907

Chinese Metallic Mirrors, New York.

Holmberg, M.S.
1946

The god Ptah, Lund.

Honoré, P.
1963

In Quest of the White God, London:

Hornell, J.
1946

Water Transport, Cambridge.

Isha, L. Schwaller de
1954

Her Bak, London.

Izikowitz, K.G.
1934, 1970

Musical and other sound instruments of the South American Indians, Wakefield, Yorkshire.

James, E.O.
1958

Myth and Ritual in the Ancient Near East, London.

1966

The Tree of Life, Leiden.

Janse, O.R.T.
1947, 1951

Archaeological Research in Indo-China, 2 vols, Cambridge, Massachusetts.

Jastrow, M.
1898

The Religion of Babylonia and Assyria.

Joralemon, P.D.
1971

A Study of Olmec Iconography, Studies in Pre-Columbian Art & Archaeology, no.7, Dumbarton Oaks, Washington, D.C.

Joyce, T.A.
1913

"The Weeping God", *Essays presented to William Ridgeway,* ed. E.C. Quiggin, pp.365-74, Cambridge.

Jairazbhoy, R.A.
1963

Foreign Influence in Ancient India, Bombay.

1971

"Egypt's Conquest of Mexico", *The Times,* 26 August, London.

1972a

"Did the Ancient Egyptians reach America?", *Illustrated London News,* August, no.6889, pp.40-1.

1972b

"The Egyptian Origin of the Olmecs" (G. Kraus), *The New Diffusionist,* pp.53-5, Sandy, Bedfordshire.

1972c

"Egyptian gods in Mexico", *XL Congresso Internazionale degli Americanisti,* 3-9 September, Rome.

Keleman, P.
1969

Medieval American Art, 3rd ed., New York.

Kelley, D.H.
1960

"Calendar animals and deities", *Southwestern Journal of Anthropology,* XVI, pp.317-37.

1966

"A cylinder seal from Tlatilco", *American Antiquity,* vol.31, no.5, pp.744-6.

126

Kern, J.H.C.
1961
"An Egyptian black pottery duck of c.1600 B.C. in Leyden", *Oudheidkundige Mededelingen*, Leiden, XLII, pp.1-6.

Kramer, S.N.
1969
"The death of Ur-Nammu and his descent to the Netherworld", *Journal of Cuneiform Studies*, vol.21 (1967), pp.104-122.

Kroeber, A.L.
1948
Anthropology, London.

Kubler, G.
1962
The Art and Architecture of Ancient America, London.

Kurath, G.P. and
Marti, S.
1964
Dances of Anahuac, New York.

Kwang-chih Chang
1963
The Archaeology of Ancient China, New Haven.

Lambert, W.G. and
Millard, A.R.
1969
Atrahasis; the Babylonian Story of the Flood.

Landstrom, B.
1970
Ships of the Pharaohs, London.

Langdon, S.H.
1905
Building Inscriptions of the Neo-Babylonian Empire, Paris.

Larco Hoyle, R.
1941
Los Cupisniques, Lima.

1966
Viru, Geneva.

Laufer, B.
1912
Jade, Chicago.

1931
"Columbus and Cathay", *Journal of the American Oriental Society*, vol.51, pp.87-103.

Leclant, J.
1954
Enquêtes sur les sacredoces . . .

Leemans, W.F.
1960
Foreign Trade in the Old Babylonian Period, Leiden.

Lefébure, E.
1878
The Book of Hades, in *Records of the Past*, ed. The Society of Biblical Archaeology, London, X. p.79-134, XII, pp.3-35.

1889
Les Hypogées Royaux de Thèbes, (Annales du Musée Guimet), vol.16).

Legrain, G.
1909
Catalogue Général Des Antiquités Égyptiennes, Statues et Statuettes, Paris.

Li Chi
1957
The Beginnings of Chinese Civilisation.

Ling Shun-Sheng
1965
"Comparative Study of the Ancient Feng-Shan and the Ziggurat of Mesopotamia", *Bulletin of the Institute of Ethnology, Academia Sinica*, no.19.

1968
"The Mound Cultures of East China and Southeastern North America", *Academia Sinica, Institute of Ethnology*, Monographs 15, pp.174-188. On this topic see now Silverberg, R.: *Moundbuilders of Ancient America*, Greenwich, Connecticut, 1968.

Loeb, E.
1923
"The blood sacrifice complex", *Memoirs of the American Anthropological Association*, no.30.

Lothrop, S.K.
1964
Treasures of Ancient America, Skira.

MacNeish, R.S. *et al.*
1970
The Prehistory of the Tehuacan Valley, Vol.III, Ceramics, Austin, Texas, and London.

MacNutt, F.A.
1908
Letters of Cortes, New York, London.

Mahieu, Jacques de
1971
Le Grand Voyage de Dieu Soleil, Edition Speciale, France.

Margain Araujo, C.R.
1945
"La Fiesta Azteca de la Cosecha Ochpanistli", *Anales de Instituto Nacional de Antropologia e Historia*, I, 1939-40, pp.157-74.

Markham, C.R.   *Royal Commentaries of the Yncas,* London.
  1869-71
  1873   *The Fables and Rites of the Yncas,* Hakluyt Society.
Marti, S.   *Instrumentos Musicales Precortesianos,* Mexico.
  1968
  1970   *Alt Amerika, Musik der Indianer in PraKolumbischer Zeit,* Leipzig.
  1971   *Manos Simbolicas,* Mexico.
Marx, E.   "Egyptian Shipping of the 18th and 19th Dynasty", *The Mariner's*
  1946   *Mirror,* vol.32, no.1, pp.21-34.
Max Muller, W.   *Egyptian Mythology,* London.
  n.d.
Medellin, Zenil, A.   "El Dios Jaguar de San Martin", *Boletin* (INAH), Mexico, no.33,
  1968   Sept., pp.9-16.
Medhurst, W.H.   tr. *Ancient China, the Shoo King or the Historical Classic,* Shanghai.
  1846
Metraux, A.   "The Native Tribes of Eastern Bolivia . . .", *Bulletin of the Bureau of*
  1943   *American Ethnological Society,* no.134.
Metropolitan Museum of Art
  1970   *Before Cortes, Sculpture of Middle America,* New York.
Mercer, S.A.B.   *Horus, Royal God of Egypt,* Grafton, Mass.
  1942
  1952   *The Pyramid Texts,* New York, London.
Montet, P.   *Tanis,* Paris.
  1942
  1958   *Everyday Life in Egypt,* London.
Moodie, R.L.   *Roentgenologic studies of Egyptian and Peruvian mummies,* (Field
  1931   Museum of Natural History, Anthropological Memoirs, III), Chicago.
Moortgat, A.   *The Art of Ancient Mesopotamia,* London and New York.
  1967
Morenz, S.   *Gott and Mensch in Alten Agypten,* Heidelberg.
  1965
Morley, S.G.   *The Ancient Maya,* Stanford, London.
  1946, 1956
Motolinia   *Motolinia's History of the Indians of New Spain,* (Cortes Society),
  1950   tr. E.A. Foster.
Murray, M.A.   *The Splendour that was Egypt,* London.
  1965
Musée du Louvre   *Le Départment des Antiquities Égyptiennés, Guide Sommaire,*
  1952   (J. Vandier), Paris.
Naville, E.   *Temple of Deir al Bahri,* Oriental Institute of Chicago, LVI.
  1901
Needham, J.   *Science and Civilisation in China,* London.
  1959, 1962, 1971
Nelson, H.H. and
  Hoelscher, U.   *Medinet Habu 1924-28,* Oriental Institute Communications no.5,
  1929   Chicago.
Neugebauer, O. and
  Parker, R.A.   *Egyptian Astronomical Texts,* I, London.
  1960
Nicholson, H.B.   "Religion in Pre-Hispanic Central Mexico", in *Handbook of Middle*
  1971   *American Indians,* vol.10, ed. R. Wauchope, Austin, Texas,
    pp.395-446.
Nicholson, I.   *Mexican and Central American Mythology,* London.
  1968
Nissen   *Orientation, Studien zur Gesehichte der Religion.*
  1906-10
Nordenskiold, E.   "Origin of the Indian civilisations in South America", *Comparative*
  1931   *Ethnographical Studies,* Goteborg, 9, pp.1-153.

128

Norman, V. Garth 1973	*Izapa Sculpture,* (New World Archaeological Foundation), Provo, Utah.
Obayashi, T. 1959	"Divination from entrails among the ancient Inca and its relations to practices in S.E. Asia", *Actas del 33 Congresso Internacional de Americanistas,* I, pp.327-332, San José.
Otto, E. 1968	*Egyptian art and the Cults of Osiris and Amon,* London.
Paton, D. 1916	*Early Egyptian Records of Travel,* Princeton.
Patterson, Thomas C. 1971	"Chavin: an interpretation of its spread and significance", *Dumbarton Oaks Conference on Chavin,* ed. E.P. Benson, Washington, D.C.
Peñafiel, A. 1900	*Teotihuacan, Estudio Historicos y Arqueologico,* Mexico.
Piankoff, A. 1934	"The sky-goddess Nut and the Night Journey of the Sun", *Journal of Egyptian Archaeology,* XX, pp.57-61.
1954	*The Tomb of Rameses VI* (Bollingen Series, XL.1), New York.
1955	*The Shrines of Tut-Ankh-Amon,* New York, (Bollingen series, XL.2).
1957	*Mythological Papyri,* (Bollingen series, XL.3), New York.
1964	*The Litany of Re,* (Bollingen series XL.4), New York.
Pitt-Rivers, J. 1970	"Spiritual Power in Central America—the Naguals of Chiapas", *Witchcraft, Confessions and Accusations,* ed. M. Douglas, London, pp.183-206.
Ponce Sanguines, C. 1972	*Tiwanaku, Espacio, Tiempo y Cultura,* La Paz.
1964	*Descripcion Sumaria del Templete Semisubterraneo di Tiwanaku,* Tiwanaku.
1970	*Procedencia del material litico de las monumentos de Tiwanaku,* La Paz, Bolivia.
Popol Vuh 1971	*The Book of Councel: The Popol Vuh of the Quiche Maya of Guatemala,* tr. Edmonson, New Orleans.
Posener, G. ed. 1962	*A Dictionary of Egyptian Civilisation,* London.
Posnansky, A. 1945, 1957	*Tihuanaco. The Cradle of American Man,* I, II, New York; III, IV, La Paz.
Pritchard, J.B. ed. 1955	*Ancient Near Eastern Texts,* Princeton.
Reichel-Dolmatoff, G. 1972	"The feline motif in Prehistoric San Agustin sculpture", *The Cult of the Feline,* ed. Benson, E.P., Dumbarton Oaks, Washington, D.C., pp.51-68.
Reiss, W. and Stubel, A. 1886-87	*The Necropolis of Ancon in Peru,* Berlin.
Remy, C. 1970	"Decouvertes Pre-Olmeques au Guatemala", *Archeologia,* no.33, Mar.-Apr. p.48.
Rickett, W.A. 1965	tr. *Kuan-Tzu, a Repository of Early Chinese Thought,* Hong Kong.
Riva Palacio, D.V. 1887	*Mexico a través de los siglos,* I, D.A. Chavero, Mexico, Barcelona.
Romero, Emilio 1967	"Existe alguna relacion entre los danzantes de Monte Alban . . .", *Selected Papers of the XXIX International Congress of Americanists,* ed. Sol Tax, Chicago.
Rosellini, I. 1832-44	*I Monumenti dell Egitto e della Nubia,* Pisa.
Rowe, J.H. 1966	"Diffusion and Archaeology", *American Antiquity,* January.
Saggs, H.W.F. 1965	*Everyday Life in Babylonia and Assyria,* London.

Sahagun, *Historia de los Cosas de Nueva Espana,* Mexico.
1829, 1946
1950-63 *Florentine Codex, General History of the Things of New Spain,* tr. A.J.O. Anderson & C.E. Dibble, Santa Fe, New Mexico, 12 books, Also Book VI, 1969.

Salas, Lorenzo Ochoa "El Culto falico y la Fertilidad en Tlatilco, Mexico", *Anales de*
1973 *Antropologia,* Mexico, X, pp.123-139.

Sandars, W.T. and
 Michels, J.W. *The Pennysylvania State University Kaminaljuyu Project, P.1, The*
1969 *Excavation.*

Save-Soderbergh, T. *The Navy of the 18th Egyptian Dynasty,* Uppsala, Leipzig.
1946

Scamuzzi, E. *Egyptian Art in the Egyptian Museum of Turin,* New York.
1965

Schafer, E.H. *Asia Major,* X, pp.77, 90.
1963

Schweitzer, H. *Das Wesen des Ka,* Hamburg.
1957

Seler, E. *The Tonalamatl of the Aubin Collection,* Berlin & London.
1900-01
1901-02 *Codex Fejervari Mayer,* Berlin, London.
1902 *Gesamelte Abhandlungen zur amerikanischer Sprach,* 4 vols.
1902-03 *Codex Vaticanus no.3773,* Berlin & London.
1906 *Codex Borgia,* Berlin, 3 vols.
1939 *Gesammelte Abhandlungen zur Amerikanischen Sprach — und Alterthumskunde,* tr. Bowditch, C.P., 4 vols, Cambridge, Mass.

Shih, C.C. "A study of Ancestor Worship in Ancient China", *The Seed of*
1964 *Wisdom",* ed. W. McCullough, pp.179-90, Toronto.

Shook, E.M. "Inventory of some pre-classic traits in the Highlands and Pacific
1971 Guatemala", *Contributions of the University of California Archaeological Research Facility,* vol.11, pp.70-77.

Shorter, A.W. *The Egyptian Gods,* London.
1937

Siren, O. *A History of Early Chinese Art, the Prehistoric and Pre Han Period,*
1929 London.
1930 *A History of Early Chinese Art — Architecture: The Han Period,* London.

Smith, S. "A Babylonian Fertility Cult", *Journal of the Royal Asiatic Society,*
1928 London, pp.849-868.

Smith, W.S. *The Art and Architecture of Ancient Egypt,* Harmondsworth.
1958

Sorenson, J.L. "Some Mesoamerican Traditions of Immigration by Sea', *El Mexico*
Dec. 1955 *Antiguo,* Mexico, VIII, pp.425-39.

Soustelle, J. *Daily Life of the Aztecs,* Harmondsworth.
1968

Spranz, B. *Die Pyramiden von Totimehuacan, Puebla (Mexico)...,* Wiesbaden.
1970

Spycket, A. "Les Statues de Culte dans les Textes Mesopotamiens...", *Cahiers de*
1968 *la Revue Biblique, 9.*

Stastny, P. "The mummy's track", *Newsweek,* November 13.
1972

Stevenson, R. *Music in Aztec and Inca territory,* University of California, Berkeley.
1968

Stewart, H.M. 1967	"Traditional Egyptian Sun Hymns of the New Kingdom", *Bulletin of the Institute of Archaeology*, no.6, London.
Stirling, M.W. 1955	"Stone Monuments of the Rio Chiquito, Veracruz, Mexico", *Smithsonian Institution Bureau of American Ethnology, Bulletin 157*, Washington, D.C., pp.1-23.
1968	*XXXVII Congresso Internacional de Americanistas*, IV, p.19f.
1968	*Dumbarton Oaks Conference on the Olmecs*, ed. E.P. Benson, Washington, D.C.
Stone, Doris 1958	*Introduction to the Archaeology of Costa Rica*, Costa Rica.
Thausing, G. and Goedicke, H. 1971	*Nofretari*, Graz, Austria.
Thomas, E. 1959	"Terrestrial marsh and Solar boat", *Journal of Egyptian Archaeology*, vol.45, pp.38-51.
Thompson, J.E.S. 1943	"Representation of Tlalchitonatiuh at Chichen Itza . . .", *Notes on Middle American Archaeology and Ethnology*, (New York), no.19, March, pp.117-21.
1957	"Deities portrayed on censers at Mayapan", *Carnegie Institute of Washington, Department of Archaeology Current Reports*, no.40, July, pp.599-632.
1960	*Maya Hieroglyphic Writing*, Norman, Oklahoma.
Tomas, A. 1971	*We are not the First*, London.
Touny, A.D. and Wenig, S. 1969	*Der Sport im Alten Agypten*, Leipzig.
Tozzer, A.M. 1941	tr. *Landa's Relacion de las Cosas de Yucatan*, Peabody Museum.
1957	"Chichen Itza and its Cenote of Sacrifice", *Memoirs of the Peabody Museum of Archaeology and Ethnology*, XI and XII, Harvard University, Cambridge, 2 vols.
Tuggle, H.D. 1968	"The Columns of El Tajin, *Ethnos*, 1-4, pp.40-70.
Ubbelohde-Doering, H. 1966	*Kulturen Alt Perus*, Tubingen.
University of Chicago 1932, 1941, 1953, 1963, etc.	*Medinet Habu*, (Oriental Institute Publications LXXXIV), Chicago.
Van Buren, E.D. 1930	*Clay figurines of Babylonia and Assyria*, London.
Von Daniken, E. 1968	*Return to the Stars*, London.
1973	*Gold of the Gods*, London.
Von Wuthenau, A. 1974	*Unexpected faces in Ancient America*, Doubleday, N.Y.
Von Hagen, V.W. 1960	*World of the Maya*, London.
Wainwright, G.A. 1934	"Some aspects of Amun", *Journal of Egyptian Archaeology*, XX, pp.139-153.
Watson, B. 1964	*Han Fei Tzu*, London, New York.
1967	*Basic Writings of Mo Tzo . . .* , New York, London.
Watson, W. 1961	*China Before the Han Dynasty*, London.
1966	*Early Civilisation in China*, London.

Wauchope, R.
1948   *Excavations of Zacualpa,* Middle American Research Institute, Publication 14, Tulane University, New Orleans.
1965   *Handbook of Middle American Indians,* vol.2, Austin, Texas.
Westropp, H.M. and
Wake, C.S.
1970   *Ancient Symbol Worship,* 3rd ed, New Delhi, (Citing Squier, *Serpent Symbol,* p.50).
Wheatley, P.
1970   "Archaeology and the Chinese City", *World Archaeology,* (London), II, no.2, October, pp.159-185.
1971   *The Pivot of the Four Quarters,* Edinburgh.
Wiercinski, A.
1969   "Ricerca antropologia sugli Olmechi", *Terra Ameriga,* nos.18-19, Rapallo. (See Juan Comas: *Anales de Antropologia,* VIII, Mexico, 1971, pp.302-4.)
Wilkinson, J.G.
1890   *A Popular Account of the Ancient Egyptians,* London.
Willey, G.
1971   "The early great styles and the rise of the PreColumbian Civilisation", *Anthropology and Art,* ed. C.M. Otten, New York.
Wilson, J.A.
1965   *The Culture of Ancient Egypt,* 10th impr., Chicago, London.
Zabkar, L.V.
1968   *A Study of the Ba Concept in Ancient Egyptian Texts,* Chicago.
Zandee, J.
1960   *Death as an Enemy,* Leiden.
1969   "The Book of Gates", *Liber Amicorum in Honour of Professor C.J. Bleeker,* Leiden.
Zuidema
1971   "Meaning in Nazca Art", *Goteborgs Etnografiken Museum,* Arstryck, pp.35-54.

2

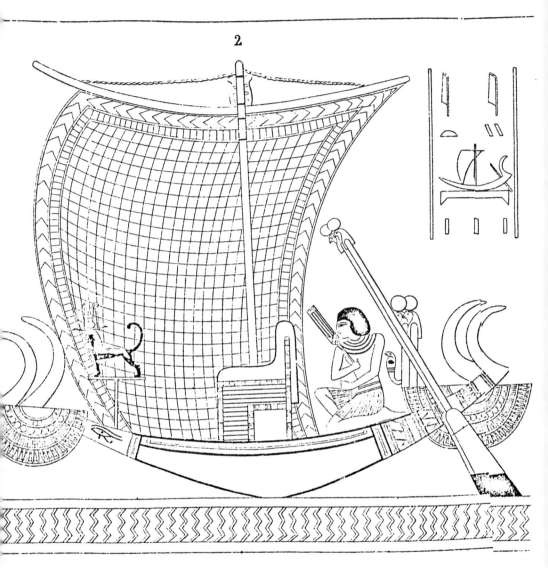

One of the ships painted in the Tomb of Rameses III. Notice hieroglyph on right with ship sailing across the sky. The figure on the ship is seated in precisely the manner of the Olmec sculpture from S. Martin illustrated on the front of the jacket of this book, also Ill. 66.

ADDENDA

For p.22 above.

This cannot be a post-Spanish interpolation because it has been observed that the same version of the legendary event of the parting of the sea recurs in most native documents (Carmack, R. M.: *Quichean Civilisation*, 1973, p.67).

For p.70 above.

It could be that the composite image of the lizard-man on the Aztec pyramid of Tenochtitlan was the last surviving vestige of Osiris, since Duran (1964, p.236) confirms that it was the god of seed-time and harvest.

For p.76.

One other point in common is that the Maya representation is on a coffin, and the Egyptian text referring to this is sometimes also on a coffin, where it says: "Thou sittest under the foilage of sweet-scented trees in the fields (of Elysium)". (Birch, S.: *Egyptian Texts of the earliest period from the Coffin of Amamu in the British Museum,* London, 1886, p.14.)

For p.95 below

It could be objected that the Tihuanaco Gate is a monolithic structure, and the Ramessid pylon is not. But on the other hand we do know that Rameses III constructed a "mysterious shrine in one block" to the sungod Ammon (Breasted, J. H.: 1906-7, IV, pp.117, 166). Another objection might be that the Tihuanaco attendant figures are winged. But once again on the Eastern Gate at Medinat Habu are attendant human figures that are winged (University of Chicago: VIII, pl.617). So repeatedly the pointer is to 12th Century B.C. Egypt, and it may be significant that one of the recent Radio Carbon dates for Tihuanaco is the 12th Century B.C. (Ponce Sanguines, C.: 1972, Table 1).

Stop Press.

On the eve of publication an important report by the anthropologist Wiercinski appeared *(see also above p.20). After examining a large number of early skulls he concludes that "A joint presence of Armenoid and Equatorial constellation of traits is typical for the Olmec populations of Mexico . . . All these exotic components in Mesoamerica came jointly from outside". And apart from the transatlantic migrants "the presence of the Pacific race in Mexico could be also related to North China of the Shang period. In this case a new transpacific migration could be accepted. Unfortunately it is impossible at present to verify this hypothesis . . . perhaps a verification will come from the cultural data".

I trust that the cultural data presented in this book fulfills that hope.

* Wiercinski, A.:K "Inter and interpopulational racial differentiation of Tlatilco,Cerro de las Mesas, Monte Alban and Yucatan Maya," *XXXIX Congresso Internacional de Americanistas Lima 1970, Actas y Memorias,* Vol. I, pp.231-252, Lima, 1972.